The Riverside Literature Series

# LAYS OF ANCIENT ROME

BY

THOMAS BABINGTON MACAULAY

*WITH THE AUTHOR'S INTRODUCTIONS, AND
ADDITIONAL EXPLANATORY NOTES*

Sout hen ou rien

The Riverside Press

59342

BOSTON NEW YORK CHICAGO

HOUGHTON MIFFLIN COMPANY

The Riverside Press Cambridge

**03572**

# EDITOR'S PREFACE.

MACAULAY'S *Lays of Ancient Rome* is something more than a bit of pastime of a famous writer, though it partakes of this character. Macaulay, like other Englishmen of his class and training, was steeped in a knowledge of classic literature and history, which he read with his eye on English history and politics. Scholarship, since his day, has become more specialized, and it is not common to find a man of letters so conversant with Roman life that he would turn easily from his ordinary work of writing modern history, for example, or literary essays, to the half-serious, half-entertaining task of composing imaginary ancient ballads. With Macaulay, Latin literature was a familiar field for recreation, and, his mind having been turned to questions upon the historic basis of early Roman legends, — a subject much discussed in his day, — he threw off these Lays, and accompanied them with introductory essays intended to establish his position upon grounds of scholarship. The entire body of Lays is, in effect, a long essay with poetic illustrations; but the illustrations appeal so directly to the imagination, and to the love of poetic narrative, that frequently they are printed separately without comment.

In preparing an edition for the use of American school-boys and school-girls, many of whom will be interested without having had any training in the classics, it has been thought best to give the prose introductions, not in full, since they contain matter incidental to the theme rather than essential, but so far forth as they serve to explain Macaulay's position, and to account for the action of the stories. In one or two instances the editor has supplemented these introductions, enclosing his additions in brackets [ ]. He has also furnished a few explanatory notes, and in preparing them he has been under obligation to an edition for schools, edited by Sir G. W. Cox, and published in London in 1884. The reader will notice that many passages which might otherwise require annotation will be made clear by an attentive study of Macaulay's introductions.

Readers who wish for fuller information about ancient Rome will find valuable help in *Ancient Rome in the Light of Recent Discoveries* and *The Ruins and Excavations of Ancient Rome* by Rodolfo Lanciani.

## CONTENTS

## ILLUSTRATIONS

# LAYS OF ANCIENT ROME.

## INTRODUCTION.

THAT what is called the history of the kings and early consuls of Rome is to a great extent fabulous, few scholars have, since the time of Beaufort, ventured to deny. It is certain that, more than three hundred and sixty years after the date ordinarily assigned for the foundation of the city, the public records were, with scarcely an exception, destroyed by the Gauls. It is certain that the oldest annals of the commonwealth were compiled more than a century and a half after the destruction of the records. It is certain, therefore, that the great Latin writers of a later period did not possess those materials without which a trustworthy account of the infancy of the republic could not possibly be framed. They own, indeed, that the chronicles to which they had access were filled with battles that were never fought, and consuls that were never inaugurated; and we have abundant proof that, in those chronicles, events of the greatest importance, such as the issue of the war with Porsena, and the issue of the war with Brennus, were grossly misrepresented. Under these circumstances a wise man will look with great suspicion on the legend which has come down to us. He will, perhaps, be inclined to regard the princes who are said to have founded the civil and religious institutions of Rome, the son of Mars, and the husband of Egeria, as mere mythological personages, of the same class with Perseus and Ixion.  As he draws nearer and nearer to the confines of authentic history, he will become less and less hard of belief.  He will admit that the most important parts of the narrative have some foundation in truth.  But he will distrust almost all the details, not only because they seldom rest on any solid evidence, but also because he will constantly detect in them, even when they are within the limits of physical possibility, that peculiar character, more easily understood than defined, which distinguishes the creations of the imagination from the realities of the world in which we live.

The early history of Rome is, indeed, far more poetical than anything else in Latin literature.  The loves of the Vestal and the God of War, the cradle laid among the reeds of Tiber, the fig-tree, the she-wolf, the shepherd's cabin, the recognition, the fratricide, the rape of the Sabines, the death of Tarpeia, the fall of Hostus Hostilius, the struggle of Mettus Curtius through the marsh, the women rushing with torn raiment and dishevelled hair between their fathers and their husbands, the nightly meetings of Numa and the Nymph by the well in the sacred grove, the fight of the three Romans and the three Albans, the purchase of the Sibylline books, the crime of Tullia, the simulated madness of Brutus, the ambiguous reply of the Delphian oracle to the Tarquins, the wrongs of Lucretia, the heroic actions of Horatius Cocles, of Scævola, and of Clœlia, the battle of Regillus won by the aid of Castor and Pollux, the defence of Cremera, the touching story of Coriolanus, the still more touching story of Virginia, the wild legend about the draining of the Alban lake, the combat between Valerius Corvus and the gigantic Gaul, are among the many instances which will at once suggest themselves to every reader.

. . . . . . . . . . .

The Latin literature which has come down to us is of later date than the commencement of the Second Punic War, and consists almost exclusively of words fashioned on Greek models. The Latin metres, heroic, elegiac, lyric, and dramatic, are of Greek origin. The best Latin epic poetry is the feeble echo of the Iliad and Odyssey. The best Latin eclogues are imitations of Theocritus. The plan of the most finished didactic poem in the Latin tongue was taken from Hesiod. The Latin tragedies are bad copies of the masterpieces of Sophocles and Euripides. The Latin comedies are free translations from Demophilus, Menander, and Apollodorus. The Latin philosophy was borrowed, without alteration, from the Portico and the Academy; and the great Latin orators constantly proposed to themselves as patterns the speeches of Demosthenes and Lysias.

But there was an earlier Latin literature, a literature truly Latin, which has wholly perished, — which had, indeed, almost perished long before those whom we are in the habit of regarding as the greatest Latin writers were born. That literature abounded with metrical romances, such as are found in every country where there is much curiosity and intelligence, but little reading and writing. All human beings, not utterly savage, long for some information about past times, and are delighted by narratives which present pictures to the eye of the mind. But it is only in very enlightened communities that books are readily accessible. Metrical composition, therefore, which, in a highly civilized nation is a mere luxury, is, in nations imperfectly civilized, almost a necessary of life, and is valued less on account of the pleasure which it gives to the ear than on account of the help which it gives to the memory. A man who can invent or embellish an interesting story, and put it into a form which others may easily retain in their recollection, will always be highly esteemed by a people eager for amusement and information, but destitute of libraries. Such is the origin of ballad-poetry, a species of composition which scarcely ever fails to spring up and flourish in every society, at a certain point in the progress towards refinement.

.        .        .        .        .        .        .        .        .

As it is agreeable to general experience that, at a certain stage in the progress of society, ballad-poetry should flourish, so is it also agreeable to general experience that, at a subsequent stage in the progress of society, ballad-poetry should be undervalued and neglected. Knowledge advances; manners change; great foreign models of composition are studied and imitated. The phraseology of the old minstrels becomes obsolete. Their versification, which, having received its laws only from the ear, abounds in irregularities, seems licentious and uncouth. Their simplicity appears beggarly when compared with the quaint forms and gaudy coloring of such artists as Cowley and Gongora. The ancient lays, unjustly despised by the learned and polite, linger for a time in the memory of the vulgar, and are at length too often irretrievably lost. We cannot wonder that the ballads of Rome should have altogether disappeared, when we remember how very narrowly, in spite of the inven-

tion of printing, those of our own country and those of
Spain escaped the same fate. There is, indeed, little
doubt that oblivion covers many English songs equal to
any that were published by Bishop Percy, and many
Spanish songs as good as the best of those which have
been so happily translated by Mr. Lockhart. Eighty
years ago England possessed only one tattered copy of
Childe Waters and Sir Cauline, and Spain only one
tattered copy of the noble poem of the Cid. The snuff
of a candle, or a mischievous dog, might in a moment
have deprived the world forever of any of those fine
compositions. Sir Walter Scott, who united to the fire
of a great poet the minute curiosity and patient dili-
gence of a great antiquary, was but just in time to save
the precious reliques of the Minstrelsy of the Border.
In Germany, the lay of the Nibelungs had been long
utterly forgotten, when, in the eighteenth century, it
was for the first time printed from a manuscript in
the old library of a noble family. In truth, the only
people who, through their whole passage from simplicity
to the highest civilization, never for a moment ceased to
love and admire their old ballads, were the Greeks.

That the early Romans should have had ballad-poetry,
and that this poetry should have perished, is, therefore,
not strange. It would, on the contrary, have been
strange if these things had not come to pass; and we
should be justified in pronouncing them highly proba-
ble, even if we had no direct evidence on the subject;
but we have direct evidence of unquestionable authority.

.   .   .   .   .   .   .   .   .   .   .

The proposition, then, that Rome had ballad-poetry
is not merely in itself highly probable, but is fully
proved by direct evidence of the greatest weight.

This proposition being established, it becomes easy to understand why the early history of the city is unlike almost everything else in Latin literature, — native where almost everything else is borrowed, imaginative where almost everything else is prosaic. We can scarcely hesitate to pronounce that the magnificent, pathetic, and truly national legends, which present so striking a contrast to all that surrounds them, are broken and defaced fragments of that early poetry which, even in the age of Cato the Censor, had become antiquated, and of which Tully had never heard a line.

That this poetry should have been suffered to perish will not appear strange when we consider how complete was the triumph of the Greek genius over the public mind of Italy. It is probable that at an early period Homer and Herodotus furnished some hints to the Latin minstrels; but it was not until after the war with Pyrrhus that the poetry of Rome began to put off its old Ausonian character. The transformation was soon consummated. The conquered, says Horace, led captive the conquerors. It was precisely at the time at which the Roman people rose to unrivalled political ascendency that they stooped to pass under the intellectual yoke. It was precisely at the time at which the sceptre departed from Greece that the empire of her language and of her arts became universal and despotic. The revolution, indeed, was not effected without a struggle. Nævius seems to have been the last of the ancient line of poets. Ennius was the founder of a new dynasty. Nævius celebrated the First Punic War in Saturnian verse, the old national verse of Italy. Ennius sang the Second Punic War in numbers borrowed from the Iliad. The elder poet, in the epitaph which he wrote for himself, and which is a fine specimen of the early Roman diction and versification, plaintively boasted that the Latin language had died with him. Thus, what to Horace appeared to be the first faint dawn of Roman literature, appeared to Nævius to be its hopeless setting. In truth, one literature was setting and another dawning.

The victory of foreign taste was decisive ; and indeed we can hardly blame the Romans for turning away with contempt from the rude lays which had delighted their fathers, and giving their whole admiration to the immortal productions of Greece. The national romances, neglected by the great and the refined, whose education had been finished at Rhodes or Athens, continued, it may be supposed, during some generations, to delight the vulgar. While Virgil, in hexameters of exquisite modulation, described the sports of rustics, those rustics were still singing their wild Saturnian ballads. It is not improbable that, at the time when Cicero lamented the irreparable loss of the poems mentioned by Cato, a search among the nooks of the Apennines, as active as the search which Sir Walter Scott made among the descendants of the mosstroopers of Liddesdale, might have brought to light many fine remains of ancient minstrelsy. No such search was made. The Latin ballads perished forever. Yet discerning critics have thought that they could still perceive in the early history of Rome numerous fragments of this lost poetry, as the traveller on classic ground sometimes finds, built into the heavy wall of a fort or convent, a pillar rich with acanthus leaves, or a frieze where the Amazons and Bacchanals seem to live. The theatres and temples of the Greek and the Roman were degraded into the quarries of the Turk and the Goth.   Even so did the ancient Saturnian poetry become the quarry in which a crowd of orators and annalists found the materials for their prose.

It is not difficult to trace the process by which the old songs were transmuted into the form which they now wear.   Funeral panegyric and chronicle appear to have been the intermediate links which connected the lost ballads with the histories now extant.   From a very early period it was the usage that an oration should be pronounced over the remains of a noble Roman.   The orator, as we learn from Polybius, was expected, on such an occasion, to recapitulate all the services which the ancestors of the deceased had, from the earliest time, rendered to the commonwealth.   There can be little doubt that the speaker on whom this duty was imposed would make use of all the stories suited to his purpose which were to be found in the popular lays. There can be little doubt that the family of an eminent man would preserve a copy of the speech which had been pronounced over his corpse.   The compilers of the early chronicles would have recourse to these speeches, and the great historians of a later period would have recourse to the chronicles.

.   .   .   .   .   .   .   .   .   .   .

Such, or nearly such, appears to have been the process by which the lost ballad-poetry of Rome was transformed into history.   To reverse that process, to transform some portions of early Roman history back into the poetry out of which they were made, is the object of this work.

In the following poems the author speaks, not in his own person, but in the persons of ancient minstrels who know only what a Roman citizen, born three or four years before the Christian era, may be supposed to have known, and who are in no wise above the passions and prejudices of their age and nation. To these imaginary poets must be ascribed some blunders, which are so obvious that it is unnecessary to point them out. The real blunder would have been to represent these old poets as deeply versed in general history, and studious of chronological accuracy. To them must also be attributed the illiberal sneers at the Greeks, the furious party spirit, the contempt for the arts of peace, the love of war for its own sake, the ungenerous exultation over the vanquished, which the reader will sometimes observe. To portray a Roman of the age of Camillus or Curius as superior to national antipathies, as mourning over the devastation and slaughter by which empire and triumphs were to be won, as looking on human suffering with the sympathy of Howard, or as treating conquered enemies with the delicacy of the Black Prince, would be to violate all dramatic propriety. The old Romans had some great virtues, — fortitude, temperance, veracity, spirit to resist oppression, respect for legitimate authority, fidelity in the observing of contracts, disinterestedness, ardent patriotism ; but Christian charity and chivalrous generosity were alike unknown to them.

It would have been obviously improper to mimic the manner of any particular age or country. Something has been borrowed, however, from our own ballads, and more from Sir Walter Scott, the great restorer of our ballad-poetry. To the Iliad still greater obligations are due ; and those obligations have been contracted with the less hesitation because there is reason to believe that some of the old Latin minstrels really had recourse to that inexhaustible store of poetical images.

# HORATIUS.

THERE can be little doubt that among those parts of early Roman history which had a poetical origin was the legend of Horatius Cocles. We have several versions of the story, and these versions differ from each other in points of no small importance. Polybius, there is reason to believe, heard the tale recited over the remains of some consul or prætor descended from the old Horatian patricians ; for he introduces it as a specimen of the narratives with which the Romans were in the habit of embellishing their funeral oratory. It is remarkable that, according to him, Horatius defended the bridge alone, and perished in the waters. According to the chronicles which Livy and Dionysius followed, Horatius had two companions, swam safe to shore, and was loaded with honors and rewards.

. . . . . . . . . . .

It is by no means unlikely that there were two old Roman lays about the defence of the bridge ; and that, while the story which Livy has transmitted to us was preferred by the multitude, the other, which ascribed the whole glory to Horatius alone, may have been the favorite with the Horatian house.

The following ballad is supposed to have been made about a hundred and twenty years after the war which it celebrates, and just before the taking of Rome by the Gauls. The author seems to have been an honest citizen, proud of the military glory of his country, sick of the disputes of factions, and much given to pining after good old times which had never really existed. The allusion, however, to the partial manner in which the public lands were allotted could proceed only from a plebeian ; and the allusion to the fraudulent sale of spoils marks the date of the poem, and shows that the poet shared in the general discontent with which the proceedings of Camillus, after the taking of Veii, were regarded.

[The legendary history makes an Etruscan dynasty of three kings, Tarquinius Priscus, Servius Tullius, and Tarquinius Superbus, to have ruled Rome successively ; but the tyranny of the house became so hateful that the Tarquinian family was banished, and a republic, governed by two magistrates called consuls, chosen annually, was set up 509 B. C., or in the year 244 from the foundation of Rome. Tarquin attempted, first by intrigue and then by open war, to recover his throne ; it was then that he sought the alliance of Porsena, who ruled over Etruria, and the ballad that follows narrates the exploit of Horatius when the city was defending itself.]

# HORATIUS.

A LAY MADE ABOUT THE YEAR OF THE CITY CCCLX

### 1

Lars Porsena of Clusium
By the Nine Gods he swore
That the great house of Tarquin
Should suffer wrong no more.
5 By the Nine Gods he swore it,
And named a trysting day,
And bade his messengers ride forth
East and west and south and north,
To summon his array.

### 2

10 East and west and south and north
The messengers ride fast,
And tower and town and cottage
Have heard the trumpet's blast.
Shame on the false Etruscan
15 Who lingers in his home,
When Porsena of Clusium
Is on the march for Rome.

### 3

The horsemen and the footmen
Are pouring in amain

1. *Lars* in the Etruscan tongue signified *chieftain. Clusium* is the modern *Jhiusi.*
2. The Romans had a tradition that there were nine great Etruscan gods.

20 From many a stately market-place;
  From many a fruitful plain;
From many a lonely hamlet,
  Which, hid by beech and pine,
Like an eagle's nest, hangs on the crest
25 Of purple Apennine;

### 4

From lordly Volaterræ,
  Where scowls the far-famed hold
Piled by the hands of giants
  For godlike kings of old;
30 From seagirt Populonia,
  Whose sentinels descry
Sardinia's snowy mountain-tops
  Fringing the southern sky;

### 5

From the proud mart of Pisæ,
35 Queen of the western waves,
Where ride Massilia's triremes
  Heavy with fair-haired slaves;
From where sweet Clanis wanders
  Through corn and vines and flowers;

26. *Volaterræ,* modern *Volterra.*
27. "The situation of the Etruscan towns is one of the most striking characteristics of Tuscan scenery. Many of them occupy surfaces of table-land surrounded by a series of gullies not visible from a distance. The traveller thus may be a whole day reaching a place which in the morning may have seemed to him but a little way off." — DENNIS, *Cities and Cemeteries of Etruria.*
34. *Pisæ,* now *Pisa.*
36. *Massilia,* the ancient *Marseilles,* which originally was a Greek colony and a great commercial centre.
37. The *fair-haired* slaves were doubtless slaves from Gaul, bought and sold by the Greek merchants.
38. *Clanis,* the modern *la Chicana.*

40 From where Cortona lifts to heaven
    Her diadem of towers.

### 6

Tall are the oaks whose acorns
    Drop in dark Auser's rill;
Fat are the stags that champ the boughs
45    Of the Ciminian hill;
Beyond all streams Clitumnus
    Is to the herdsman dear;
Best of all pools the fowler loves
    The great Volsinian mere.

### 7

50 But now no stroke of woodman
    Is heard by Auser's rill;
No hunter tracks the stag's green path
    Up the Ciminian hill;
Unwatched along Clitumnus
55    Grazes the milk-white steer;
Unharmed the waterfowl may dip
    In the Volsinian mere.

### 8

The harvests of Arretium,
    This year, old men shall reap,
60 This year, young boys in Umbro

43. The *Auser* was a tributary stream of the river *Arno*.
46. *Clitumnus, Clituno* in modern times.
49. *Volsinian mere*, now known as *Lago di Bolsena.*
58. *Arretium*, now *Arezzo.*
60. *Umbro*, the river *Ombrone*. All this region was occupied by the Etrus-
cans, and since the men had gone to fight Rome, only the old and very
young would be left to carry on the work of the country.

Shall plunge the struggling sheep;
And in the vats of Luna,
    This year, the must shall foam
Round the white feet of laughing girls
**65**    Whose sires have marched to **Rome.**

### 9

There be thirty chosen prophets,
    The wisest of the land,
Who alway by Lars Porsena
    Both morn and evening stand:
**70** Evening and morn the Thirty
    Have turned the verses o'er,
Traced from the right on linen white
    By mighty seers of yore.

### 10

And with one voice the Thirty
**75**    Have their glad answer given:
" Go forth, go forth, Lars Porsena;
    Go forth, beloved of Heaven:
Go, and return in glory
    To Clusium's royal dome;
**80** And hang round Nurscia's altars
    The golden shields of Rome."

### 11

And now hath every city
    Sent up her tale of men:

66. The Etruscan religion was one of sorcery, and their prophets were augurs who sought to know the will of the gods by various outward signs; such as the flight of birds, the direction of lightning, and the mystic writings of the prophets before them.

72. The Etruscan writing was from right to left.

83. *Tale of men.* Compare Milton's lines in *L'Allegro,* —

The foot are fourscore thousand,
85   The horse are thousands ten.
Before the gates of Sutrium
     Is met the great array.
A proud man was Lars Porsena
     Upon the trysting day.

### 12

90 For all the Etruscan armies
     Were ranged beneath his eye,
And many a banished Roman,
     And many a stout ally;
And with a mighty following
95   To join the muster came
The Tusculan Mamilius,
     Prince of the Latian name.

### 13

But by the yellow Tiber
     Was tumult and affright:
100 From all the spacious champaign
     To Rome men took their flight.
A mile around the city,
     The throng stopped up the ways;
A fearful sight it was to see
105   Through two long nights and days.

### 14

For aged folks on crutches,
     And women great with child,

" And every shepherd tells his tale
      Under the hawthorn, in the dale."
The *tally* which we keep is a kindred word.
86. *Sutrium* is *Sutri* to-day.

And mothers sobbing over babes
　　That clung to them and smiled,
110 And sick men borne in litters
　　High on the necks of slaves,
And troops of sunburnt husbandmen
　　With reaping-hooks and staves,

### 15

And droves of mules and asses
115　Laden with skins of wine,
And endless flocks of goats and sheep,
　　And endless herds of kine,
And endless trains of wagons
　　That creaked beneath the weight
120 Of corn-sacks and of household goods,
　　Choked every roaring gate.

### 16

Now, from the rock Tarpeian,
　　Could the wan burghers spy
The line of blazing villages
125　Red in the midnight sky.
The Fathers of the City,
　　They sat all night and day,
For every hour some horseman came
　　With tidings of dismay.

### 17

130 To eastward and to westward
　　Have spread the Tuscan bands;

122. The Tarpeian rock was a cliff on the steepest side of the Capitoline
Hill in Rome, and overhung the Tiber.
123. *Burghers.* Macaulay uses a very modern word to describe the men
of Rome.
126. *The Fathers of the City,* otherwise the Senators of Rome.

Nor house nor fence nor dovecote
    In Crustumerium stands.
Verbenna down to Ostia
135    Hath wasted all the plain ;
Astur hath stormed Janiculum,
    And the stout guards are slain.

### 18

Iwis, in all the Senate,
    There was no heart so bold,
140 But sore it ached, and fast it beat,
    When that ill news was told.
Forthwith up rose the Consul,
    Up rose the Fathers all ;
In haste they girded up their gowns,
145    And hied them to the wall.

### 19

They held a council standing
    Before the River-Gate ;
Short time was there, ye well may guess,
    For musing or debate.
150 Out spake the Consul roundly :
    " The bridge must straight go down ;
For, since Janiculum is lost,
    Naught else can save the town."

---

134. *Ostia*, at the mouth of the Tiber, was the port of Rome.
136. The Janiculan hill was on the right bank of the Tiber.
138. *Iwis.* Compare Lowell's lines in *Credidimus Jovem regnare : —*

> " God vanished long ago, iwis,
>     A mere subjective synthesis."

Its meaning is " certainly."
151. The *bridge* was the Sublician bridge, said to have been thrown across the Tiber by Ancus Martius in the year 114 of the city.

### 20

Just then a scout came flying,
155    All wild with haste and fear;
"To arms! to arms! Sir Consul:
Lars Porsena is here."
On the low hills to westward
The Consul fixed his eye,
160 And saw the swarthy storm of dust
Rise fast along the sky.

### 21

And nearer fast and nearer
Doth the red whirlwind come;
And louder still and still more loud,
165 From underneath that rolling cloud,
Is heard the trumpet's war-note proud,
The trampling, and the hum.
And plainly and more plainly
Now through the gloom appears,
170 Far to left and far to right,
In broken gleams of dark-blue light,
The long array of helmets bright,
The long array of spears.

### 22

And plainly, and more plainly
175    Above that glimmering line,
Now might ye see the banners
Of twelve fair cities shine;
But the banner of proud Clusium
Was highest of them all,

177. The Etruscan confederacy was composed of twelve cities.

**180** The terror of the Umbrian,
> The terror of the Gaul.

### 23

And plainly and more plainly
> Now might the burghers know,
By port and vest, by horse and crest,
**185**   Each warlike Lucumo.
> There Cilnius of Arretium
>> On his fleet roan was seen ;
> And Astur of the fourfold shield,
> Girt with the brand none else may wield,
**190** Tolumnius with the belt of gold,
> And dark Verbenna from the hold
>> By reedy Thrasymene.

### 24

Fast by the royal standard,
> O'erlooking all the war,
**195** Lars Porsena of Clusium
> Sat in his ivory car.
By the right wheel rode Mamilius,
> Prince of the Latian name ;
And by the left false Sextus,
**200**   That wrought the deed of shame.

---

184. By *port and vest*, i. e., by the way he carried himself and by his dress. *Vest*, an abbreviation of vesture.

185. *Lucumo* was the name given by the Latin writers to the Etruscan chiefs.

192. *Thrasymene* or *Trasimenus* is *Lago di Perugia*, and was famous in Roman history as the scene of a victory by Hannibal, the Carthaginian general, over the Roman forces.

197. Octavius Mamilius of Tusculum married the daughter of Tarquinius.

199. Sextus, a son of Tarquinius, and the one whose wickedness was the immediate cause of the expulsion of the Tarquins.

### 25

But when the face of Sextus
 Was seen among the foes,
A yell that rent the firmament
 From all the town arose.
205 On the house-tops was no woman
  But spat towards him and hissed,
No child but screamed out curses,
 And shook its little fist.

### 26

But the Consul's brow was sad,
210 And the Consul's speech was low,
And darkly looked he at the wall,
 And darkly at the foe.
"Their van will be upon us
 Before the bridge goes down;
215 And if they once may win the bridge,
 What hope to save the town?"

### 27

Then out spake brave Horatius,
 The Captain of the Gate:
"To every man upon this earth
220 Death cometh soon or late;
And how can man die better
 Than facing fearful odds,
For the ashes of his fathers,
 And the temples of his Gods,

### 28

225 "And for the tender mother
 Who dandled him to rest,

And for the wife who nurses
His baby at her breast,
And for the holy maidens
**230** Who feed the eternal flame,
To save them from false Sextus
That wrought the deed of shame?

## 29

"Hew down the bridge, Sir Consul,
With all the speed ye may;
**235** I, with two more to help me,
Will hold the foe in play.
In yon strait path a thousand
May well be stopped by three.
Now who will stand on either hand,
**240** And keep the bridge with me?"

## 30

Then out spake Spurius Lartius;
A Ramnian proud was he:
"Lo, I will stand at thy right hand,
And keep the bridge with thee."
**245** And out spake strong Herminius;
Of Titian blood was he:
"I will abide on thy left side,
And keep the bridge with thee."

229. The Vestal Virgins were bound by vows of celibacy, and kept burning the sacred fire of Vesta. The order survived till near the close of the fourth century of our era. For a very interesting account of the House of the Vestal Virgins, see LANCIANI, *Ancient Rome in the Light of Recent Discoveries.*

242. The *Ramnes* were one of the three tribes who comprised the Roman Patricians, or noble class.

246. The *Tities* were another of these three tribes.

## 31

"Horatius," quoth the Consul,
250    "As thou sayest, so let it be."
    And straight against that great array
        Forth went the dauntless Three.
    For Romans in Rome's quarrel
        Spared neither land nor gold,
255 Nor son nor wife, nor limb nor life,
        In the brave days of old.

## 32

    Then none was for a party;
        Then all were for the state;
    Then the great man helped the poor,
260     And the poor man loved the great:
    Then lands were fairly portioned;
        Then spoils were fairly sold:
    The Romans were like brothers
        In the brave days of old.

## 33

265 Now Roman is to Roman
        More hateful than a foe,
    And the Tribunes beard the high,
        And the Fathers grind the low.
    As we wax hot in faction,
270     In battle we wax cold:
    Wherefore men fight not as they fought
        In the brave days of old.

267. The *Tribunes* were officers who represented the tribes of the common people or *Plebs* of Rome. In the time when the ballad is supposed to be written, there were two strong parties, the Fathers or Patricians (*Patres*), the Common People or Plebs.

### 34

Now while the Three were tightening
    Their harness on their backs,
275 The Consul was the foremost man
    To take in hand an axe:
And Fathers mixed with Commons
    Seized hatchet, bar, and crow,
And smote upon the planks above,
280    And loosed the props below.

### 35

Meanwhile the Tuscan army,
    Right glorious to behold,
Came flashing back the noonday light,
Rank behind rank, like surges bright
285    Of a broad sea of gold.
Four hundred trumpets sounded
    A peal of warlike glee,
As that great host, with measured tread,
And spears advanced, and ensigns spread,
290 Rolled slowly towards the bridge's head,
    Where stood the dauntless Three.

### 36

The Three stood calm and silent,
    And looked upon the foes,
And a great shout of laughter
295    From all the vanguard rose ;
And forth three chiefs came spurring
    Before that deep array ;

---

277. *Commons.* Macaulay, an English Whig, used a political word very
dear to him, as representing the rise of English parliamentary government.

280. The *props* held up the bridge from below. The Latin word for props
was *sublicæ ;* hence the Sublician bridge.

To earth they sprang, their swords they drew,
And lifted high their shields, and flew
**300**    To win the narrow way;

### 37

Aunus from green Tifernum,
    Lord of the Hill of Vines;
And Seius, whose eight hundred slaves
    Sicken in Ilva's mines;
**305** And Picus, long to Clusium
    Vassal in peace and war,
Who led to fight his Umbrian powers
From that gray crag where, girt with towers,
The fortress of Nequinum lowers
**310**    O'er the pale waves of Nar.

### 38

Stout Lartius hurled down Aunus
    Into the stream beneath:
Herminius struck at Seius,
    And clove him to the teeth:
**315** At Picus brave Horatius
    Darted one fiery thrust;
And the proud Umbrian's gilded arms
    Clashed in the bloody dust.

### 39

Then Ocnus of Falerii
**320**    Rushed on the Roman Three;

301. *Tifernum* was on the west side of the Apennines, near the source of the Tiber.   It is now *Città di Castello.*

304. *Ilva* is the modern *Elba,* renowned as the island to which Napoleon was banished.

309. *Nequinum,* afterward *Narnia* and now *Narni,* on the banks of the Nar.

And Lausulus of Urgo,
    The rover of the sea ;
And Aruns of Volsinium,
    Who slew the great wild boar,
325 The great wild boar that had his den
Amidst the reeds of Cosa's fen,
And wasted fields, and slaughtered men,
    Along Albinia's shore.

### 40

Herminius smote down Aruns :
330    Lartius laid Ocnus low :
Right to the heart of Lausulus
    Horatius sent a blow.
" Lie there," he cried, "fell pirate !
    No more, aghast and pale,
335 From Ostia's walls the crowd shall mark
The track of thy destroying bark.
No more Campania's hinds shall fly
To woods and caverns when they spy
    Thy thrice accursed sail."

### 41

340 But now no sound of laughter
    Was heard among the foes.
A wild and wrathful clamor
    From all the vanguard rose.
Six spears' lengths from the entrance
345    Halted that deep array,
And for a space no man came forth
    To win the narrow way.

322. The Etruscans were pirates as well as merchants.

### 42

But hark! the cry is Astur:
    And lo! the ranks divide;
350 And the great Lord of Luna
    Comes with his stately stride.
Upon his ample shoulders
    Clangs loud the fourfold shield,
And in his hand he shakes the brand
355     Which none but he can wield.

### 43

He smiled on those bold Romans
    A smile serene and high;
He eyed the flinching Tuscans,
    And scorn was in his eye.
360 Quoth he, "The she-wolf's litter
    Stand savagely at bay:
But will ye dare to follow,
    If Astur clears the way?"

### 44

Then, whirling up his broadsword
365     With both hands to the height,
He rushed against Horatius,
    And smote with all his might.
With shield and blade Horatius
    Right deftly turned the blow.
370 The blow, though turned, came yet too nigh;
    It missed his helm, but gashed his thigh:
The Tuscans raised a joyful cry
    To see the red blood flow.

360. The *she-wolf's litter*. The reference is to the story of the suckling of Romulus and Remus by a she-wolf.

### 45

He reeled, and on Herminius
375    He leaned one breathing-space;
Then, like a wild-cat mad with wounds,
    Sprang right at Astur's face.
Through teeth, and skull, and helmet,
    So fierce a thrust he sped,
380 The good sword stood a handbreadth out
    Behind the Tuscan's head.

### 46

And the great Lord of Luna
    Fell at that deadly stroke,
As falls on Mount Alvernus
385    A thunder-smitten oak.
Far o'er the crashing forest
    The giant arms lie spread;
And the pale augurs, muttering low,
    Gaze on the blasted head.

### 47

390 On Astur's throat Horatius
    Right firmly pressed his heel,
And thrice and four times tugged amain,
    Ere he wrenched out the steel.
" And see," he cried, " the welcome,
395    Fair guests, that waits you here!
What noble Lucumo comes next
    To taste our Roman cheer ? "

### 48

But at his haughty challenge
    A sullen murmur ran,

400 Mingled of wrath and shame and dread,
    Along that glittering van.
There lacked not men of prowess,
    Nor men of lordly race;
For all Etruria's noblest
405    Were round the fatal place.

### 49

But all Etruria's noblest
    Felt their hearts sink to see
On the earth the bloody corpses,
    In the path the dauntless Three:
410 And, from the ghastly entrance
    Where those bold Romans stood,
All shrank, like boys who unaware,
Ranging the woods to start a hare,
Come to the mouth of the dark lair
415 Where, growling low, a fierce old bear
    Lies amidst bones and blood.

### 50

Was none who would be foremost
    To lead such dire attack:
But those behind cried " Forward ! "
420    And those before cried "Back ! "
And backward now and forward
    Wavers the deep array;
And on the tossing sea of steel,
To and fro the standards reel;
425 And the victorious trumpet-peal
    Dies fitfully away

### 51

Yet one man for one moment
  Stood out before the crowd;
Well known was he to all the Three,
430   And they gave him greeting loud,
  " Now welcome, welcome, Sextus!
  Now welcome to thy home!
Why dost thou stay, and turn away?
  Here lies the road to Rome."

### 52

435 Thrice looked he at the city;
  Thrice looked he at the dead;
And thrice came on in fury,
  And thrice turned back in dread;
And, white with fear and hatred,
440   Scowled at the narrow way
Where, wallowing in a pool of blood,
  The bravest Tuscans lay.

### 53

But meanwhile axe and lever
  Have manfully been plied;
445 And now the bridge hangs tottering
  Above the boiling tide.
  " Come back, come back, Horatius!"
  Loud cried the Fathers all.
  " Back, Lartius! back, Herminius!
450   Back, ere the ruin fall!"

### 54

Back darted Spurius Lartius;
  Herminius darted back:

And, as they passed, beneath their feet
    They felt the timbers crack.
455 But when they turned their faces,
    And on the farther shore
Saw brave Horatius stand alone,
    They would have crossed once more.

### 55

But with a crash like thunder
460     Fell every loosened beam,
And, like a dam, the mighty wreck
    Lay right athwart the stream;
And a long shout of triumph
    Rose from the walls of Rome,
465 As to the highest turret-tops
    Was splashed the yellow foam.

### 56

And, like a horse unbroken
    When first he feels the rein,
The furious river struggled hard,
470     And tossed his tawny mane,
And burst the curb, and bounded,
    Rejoicing to be free,
And whirling down, in fierce career,
Battlement, and plank, and pier,
475     Rushed headlong to the sea.

### 57

Alone stood brave Horatius,
    But constant still in mind;
Thrice thirty thousand foes before,
    And the broad flood behind.

480 " Down with him ! " cried false Sextus,
    With a smile on his pale face.
" Now yield thee," cried Lars Porsena,
    " Now yield thee to our grace."

### 58

Round turned he, as not deigning
485     Those craven ranks to see ;
Naught spake he to Lars Porsena,
    To Sextus naught spake he ;
But he saw on Palatinus
    The white porch of his home ;
490 And he spake to the noble river
    That rolls by the towers of Rome.

### 59

" O Tiber ! father Tiber !
    To whom the Romans pray,
A Roman's life, a Roman's arms,
495     Take thou in charge this day ! "
So he spake, and speaking sheathed
    The good sword by his side,
And with his harness on his back
    Plunged headlong in the tide.

### 60

500 No sound of joy or sorrow
    Was heard from either bank ;
But friends and foes in dumb surprise,
With parted lips and straining eyes,
    Stood gazing where he sank ;
505 And when above the surges

488. *Mons Palatinus* survives in the Palatine hill of modern Rome.

And when above the surges
    They saw his crest appear,
All Rome sent forth a rapturous cry,
And even the ranks of Tuscany
    Could scarce forbear to cheer.

From drawing by George Scharf, Jr., in "Lays of Ancient Rome," by permission of the publishers, Messrs. Longmans, Green & Co.

They saw his crest appear,
All Rome sent forth a rapturous cry,
And even the ranks of Tuscany
 Could scarce forbear to cheer.

### 61

510 But fiercely ran the current,
 Swollen high by months of rain:
And fast his blood was flowing,
 And he was sore in pain,
And heavy with his armor,
515  And spent with changing blows:
And oft they thought him sinking,
 But still again he rose.

### 62

Never, I ween, did swimmer,
 In such an evil case,
520 Struggle through such a raging flood
 Safe to the landing-place:
But his limbs were borne up bravely
 By the brave heart within,
And our good father Tiber
525  Bore bravely up his chin.

---

525. Macaulay notes as passages in English literature which he had in mind when he wrote this:—
  " Our ladye bare upp her chinne."
           *Ballad of Childe Waters.*
  " Never heavier man and horse
   Stemmed a midnight torrent's force;
   .  .  .  .  .  .
   Yet, through good heart and our Lady's grace,
   At length he gained the landing-place."
           *Lay of the Last Minstrel.*

### 63

" Curse on him ! " quoth false Sextus ;
　" Will not the villain drown ?
But for this stay, ere close of day
　We should have sacked the town ! "
530 " Heaven help him ! " quoth Lars Porsena,
　" And bring him safe to shore ;
For such a gallant feat of arms
　Was never seen before."

### 64

And now he feels the bottom ;
535　Now on dry earth he stands ;
Now round him throng the Fathers
　To press his gory hands ;
And now, with shouts and clapping,
　And noise of weeping loud,
540 He enters through the River-Gate,
　Borne by the joyous crowd.

### 65

They gave him of the corn-land,
　That was of public right,
As much as two strong oxen
545　Could plough from morn till night ;
And they made a molten image,
　And set it up on high,
And there it stands unto this day
　To witness if I lie.

## 66

550 It stands in the Comitium,
    Plain for all folk to see;
Horatius in his harness,
    Halting upon one knee:
And underneath is written,
555     In letters all of gold,
How valiantly he kept the bridge
    In the brave days of old.

## 67

And still his name sounds stirring
    Unto the men of Rome,
560 As the trumpet-blast that cries to them
    To charge the Volscian home;
And wives still pray to Juno
    For boys with hearts as bold
As his who kept the bridge so well
565     In the brave days of old.

## 68

And in the nights of winter,
    When the cold north-winds blow,
And the long howling of the wolves
    Is heard amidst the snow;
570 When round the lonely cottage
    Roars loud the tempest's din,
And the good logs of Algidus
    Roar louder yet within;

550. The *Comitium* was that part of the Forum which served as the meeting-place of the Roman patricians.

573. The Romans brought some of their firewood from the hill of Algidus, about a dozen miles to the southeast of the town.

### 69

When the oldest cask is opened,
575　And the largest lamp is lit;
When the chestnuts glow in the embers,
And the kid turns on the spit;
When young and old in circle
Around the firebrands close;
580 When the girls are weaving baskets,
And the lads are shaping bows;

### 70

When the goodman mends his armor,
And trims his helmet's plume;
When the goodwife's shuttle merrily
585　Goes flashing through the loom, —
With weeping and with laughter
Still is the story told,
How well Horatius kept the bridge
In the brave days of old.

# THE BATTLE OF THE LAKE REGILLUS.

THE following poem is supposed to have been produced ninety years after the lay of Horatius. Some persons mentioned in the lay of Horatius make their appearance again, and some appellations and epithets used in the lay of Horatius have been purposely repeated; for, in an age of ballad-poetry, it scarcely ever fails to happen, that certain phrases come to be appropriated to certain men and things, and are regularly applied to those men and things by every minstrel.

. . . . . . . . . . .

The principal distinction between the lay of Horatius and the lay of the Lake Regillus is, that the former is meant to be purely Roman, while the latter, though national in its general spirit, has a slight tincture of Greek learning and of Greek superstition. The story of the Tarquins, as it has come down to us, appears to have been compiled from the works of several popular poets; and one at least of those poets appears to have visited the Greek colonies in Italy, if not Greece itself, and to have had some acquaintance with the works of Homer and Herodotus. Many of the most striking adventures of the house of Tarquin, before Lucretia makes her appearance, have a Greek character. . . . The Battle of the Lake Regillus is in all respects a Homeric battle, except that the combatants ride astride on their horses, instead of driving chariots. The mass of fighting men is hardly mentioned. The leaders single each other out, and engage hand to hand. The great object of the warriors on both sides is, as in the Iliad, to obtain possession of the spoils and bodies of the slain ; and several circumstances are related which forcibly remind us of the great slaughter round the corpses of Sarpedon and Patroclus.

. . . . . . . . . . .

In the following poem, therefore, images and incidents have been borrowed, not merely without scruple, but on principle, from the incomparable battle-pieces of Homer.

The popular belief at Rome, from an early period, seems to have been that the event of the great day of Regillus was decided by supernatural agency. Castor and Pollux, it was said, had fought, armed and mounted, at the head of the legions of the commonwealth, and had afterwards carried the news of the victory with incredible speed to the city. The well in the Forum at which they had alighted was pointed out. Near the well rose their ancient temple. A great festival was kept to their honor on the ides of Quintilis, supposed to be the anniversary of the battle ; and on that day sumptuous sacrifices were offered to them at the public charge. One spot on the margin of Lake Regillus was regarded during many ages with superstitious awe. A mark, resembling in shape a horse's hoof, was discernible in the volcanic rock ; and this mark was believed to have been made by one of the celestial chargers.

How the legend originated cannot now be ascertained : but we may easily imagine several ways in which it might have originated ; nor is it at all necessary to suppose, with Julius Frontinus, that two young men were dressed up by the Dictator to personate the sons of Leda. It is probable that Livy is correct when he says that the Roman general, in the hour of peril, vowed a temple to Castor. If so, nothing could be more natural than that the multitude should ascribe the victory to the favor of the Twin Gods. When such was the prevailing sentiment, any man who chose to declare that, in the midst of the confusion and slaughter, he had seen two godlike forms on white horses scattering the Latines, would find ready credence. We know, indeed, that in modern times a very similar story actually found credence among a people much more civilized than the Romans of the fifth century before Christ. A chaplain of Cortes, writing about thirty years after the conquest of Mexico, in an age of printing-presses, libraries, universities, scholars, logicians, jurists, and statesmen, had the face to assert that in one engagement against the Indians St. James had appeared on a grey horse at the head of the Castilian adventurers. Many of these adventurers were living when this lie was printed. One of them, honest Bernal Diaz, wrote an account of the expedition. He had the evidence of his own senses against the legend ; but he seems to have distrusted even the evidence of his own senses. He says that he was in the battle, and that he saw a gray horse with a man on his back, but that the man was, to his thinking, Francesco de Morla, and not the ever-blessed apostle St. James. "Nevertheless," Bernal adds, " it may be that the person on the grey horse was the glorious apostle St. James, and that I, sinner that I am, was unworthy to see him." The Romans of the age of Cincinnatus were probably quite as credulous as the Spanish subjects of Charles the Fifth. It is therefore conceivable that the appearance of Castor and Pollux may have become an article of faith before the generation which had fought at Regillus had passed away. Nor could anything be more natural than that the poets of the next age should embellish this story, and make the celestial horsemen bear the tidings of victory to Rome. . . . It was ordained that a grand muster and inspection of the equestrian body [the knights of Rome] should be part of the ceremonial performed on the anniversary of the battle of Regillus in honor of Castor and Pollux, the two equestrian gods. All the knights, clad in purple and crowned with olive, were to meet at a Temple of Mars in the suburbs. Thence they were to ride in state to the Forum, where the Temple of the Twins stood. This pageant was, during several centuries, considered as one of the most splendid sights of Rome. In the time of Dionysius the cavalcade sometimes consisted of five thousand horsemen, all persons of fair repute and easy fortune.

There can be no doubt that the Censors, who instituted this august ceremony, acted in concert with the Pontiffs, to whom, by the constitution of Rome, the superintendence of the public worship belonged ; and it is probable that those high religious functionaries were, as usual, fortunate enough to find in their books or traditions some warrant for the innovation. The following poem was supposed to have been made for this great occasion.

[The battle of Lake Regillus was the last attempt of the Tarquins to regain their supremacy in Rome. Tarquin applied to his son-in-law, Octavius Mamilius of Tusculum, to aid him. A confederacy of thirty Latin cities supported him, and Rome, which called itself Latin, thus had the appearance of being in revolt. The Romans appointed Aulus Posthumius dictator, and their victory over the confederacy marked the beginning of the Roman supremacy in Italy.]

# THE BATTLE OF THE LAKE REGILLUS.

A LAY SUNG AT THE FEAST OF CASTOR AND POLLUX
ON THE IDES OF QUINTILIS, IN THE YEAR OF THE
CITY CCCCLI.

## 1

Ho, trumpets, sound a war-note!
Ho, lictors, clear the way!
The Knights will ride in all their pride
Along the streets to-day.
5 To-day the doors and windows
Are hung with garlands all,
From Castor in the Forum
To Mars without the wall.
Each Knight is robed in purple,
10 With olive each is crowned;
A gallant war-horse under each
Paws haughtily the ground.
While flows the Yellow River,
While stands the Sacred Hill,
15 The proud Ides of Quintilis
Shall have such honor still.
Gay are the Martian Kalends:

2. The *lictors* were the body-guard of the magistrates, and were armed
with rods and axes.
3. Macaulay gives a modern name to members of the Roman order, who
might be said to correspond with the Knights of the Order of St. George.
7. That is, from the Temple of Castor within the Forum to the Temple of
Mars.
13. The yellow Tiber, from the yellow sands which colored the water.
15. The Roman year began with March. *Quintilis*, the fifth month, was
therefore July; the *Ides* was the middle of the month.
17. The *Kalends* was the first day of the month. On the first of March

December's Nones are gay:
But the proud Ides, when the squadron rides,
20    Shall be Rome's whitest day.

### 2

Unto the Great Twin Brethren
We keep this solemn feast.
Swift, swift, the Great Twin Brethren
Came spurring from the east.
25 They came o'er wild Parthenius,
Tossing in waves of pine,
O'er Cirrha's dome, o'er Adria's foam,
O'er purple Apennine,
From where with flutes and dances
30    Their ancient mansion rings,
In lordly Lacedæmon,
The City of two kings,
To where, by Lake Regillus,
Under the Porcian height,

---

the sacred fire was rekindled on the hearth of the Temple of Vesta. It was New Year's Day, and one of festivity.

18. *December's Nones*, the fifth of December.

21. *The Great Twin Brethren*, Castor and Pollux, were the Box and Cox of ancient mythology. They are held by some to have represented the alternation of sun and moon.

25. *They came o'er wild Parthenius.* "These lines describe the course of the mysterious riders from their Eastern birthplace. The Parthenian range is the eastern barrier of the Arkadian or central highlands of the Peloponnese. Cirrha was the port on the Corinthian gulf for the landing of pilgrims for the great shrine of Delphi. Adria or Hadria was the name by which the Romans spoke of the Adriatic Sea; and the Apennines formed the backbone of Italy, which the twin riders had to cross before they could reach Rome." — Cox.

31. Sparta, the city of the Lacedæmonians, was said to be the city of Castor and Pollux, who were sometimes spoken of as the brothers of Helen, wife of Menelaus, the chieftain of the Lacedæmonians.

32. Anciently there were two heads of the Spartan state.

35 All in the lands of Tusculum,
  Was fought the glorious fight.

### 3

  Now on the place of slaughter
   Are cots and sheepfolds seen,
  And rows of vines, and fields of wheat,
40   And apple-orchards green ;
  The swine crush the big acorns
   That fall from Corne's oaks.
  Upon the turf by the Fair Fount
   The reaper's pottage smokes.
45 The fisher baits his angle ;
   The hunter twangs his bow ;
  Little they think on those strong limbs
   That moulder deep below.
  Little they think how sternly
50   That day the trumpets pealed ;
  How in the slippery swamp of blood
   Warrior and war-horse reeled ;
  How wolves came with fierce gallop,
   And crows on eager wings,
55 To tear the flesh of captains,
   And peck the eyes of kings ;
  How thick the dead lay scattered
   Under the Porcian height ;
  How through the gates of Tusculum
60   Raved the wild stream of flight ;
  And how the Lake Regillus
   Bubbled with crimson foam,
  What time the Thirty Cities
   Came forth to war with Rome.

*Tusculum* was near the modern *Frascati*, and stood on the height named Alba Longa.

4

65 But, Roman, when thou standest
     Upon that holy ground,
   Look thou with heed on the dark rock
     That girds the dark lake round,
   So shalt thou see a hoof-mark
70   Stamped deep into the flint:
   It was no hoof of mortal steed
     That made so strange a dint:
   There to the Great Twin Brethren
     Vow thou thy vows, and pray
75 That they, in tempest and in fight,
     Will keep thy head alway.

5

   Since last the Great Twin Brethren
     Of mortal eyes were seen,
   Have years gone by an hundred
80   And fourscore and thirteen.
   That summer a Virginius
     Was Consul first in place;
   The second was stout Aulus,
     Of the Posthumian race.
85 The Herald of the Latines
     From Gabii came in state:
   The Herald of the Latines
     Passed through Rome's Eastern Gate:
   The Herald of the Latines
90   Did in our Forum stand;
   And there he did his office,
     A sceptre in his hand.

### 6

" Hear, Senators and people
　　Of the good town of Rome,
95 The Thirty Cities charge you
　　To bring the Tarquins home ;
And if ye still be stubborn,
　　To work the Tarquins wrong,
The Thirty Cities warn you,
100　　Look that your walls be strong."

### 7

Then spake the Consul Aulus,
　　He spake a bitter jest :
" Once the jays sent a message
　　Unto the eagle's nest :
105 Now yield thou up thine eyrie
　　Unto the carrion-kite,
Or come forth valiantly, and face
　　The jays in mortal fight.
Forth looked in wrath the eagle ;
110　　And carrion-kite and jay,
Soon as they saw his beak and claw
　　Fled screaming far away."

### 8

The Herald of the Latines
　　Hath hied him back in state ;
115 The Fathers of the City
　　Are met in high debate.
Thus spake the elder Consul,
　　An ancient man and wise :

" Now hearken, Conscript Fathers,
120   To that which I advise.
In seasons of great peril
   'T is good that one bear sway;
Then choose we a Dictator,
   Whom all men shall obey.
125 Camerium knows how deeply
   The sword of Aulus bites,
And all our city calls him
   The man of seventy fights.
Then let him be Dictator
130   For six months and no more,
And have a Master of the Knights,
   And axes twenty-four."

### 9

So Aulus was Dictator,
   The man of seventy fights;
135 He made Æbutius Elva
   His Master of the Knights.
On the third morn thereafter,
   At dawning of the day,
Did Aulus and Æbutius
140   Set forth with their array.
Sempronius Atratinus
   Was left in charge at home
With boys, and with gray-headed men,
   To keep the walls of Rome.
145 Hard by the Lake Regillus
   Our camp was pitched at night;

---

119. The *Conscript Fathers* were those members of the Patrician (*patres*)
order whose names were written down (*conscripti*) in the Senate roll.

132. Each of the two Consuls had twelve Lictors. The Dictator was now
to have all of these.

Eastward a mile the Latines lay,
    Under the Porcian height.
Far over hill and valley
**150**    Their mighty host was spread ;
And with their thousand watch-fires
    The midnight sky was red.

### 10

Up rose the golden morning
    Over the Porcian height,
**155** The proud Ides of Quintilis
    Marked evermore with white.
Not without secret trouble
    Our bravest saw the foes ;
For girt by threescore thousand spears.
**160**    The thirty standards rose.
From every warlike city
    That boasts the Latian name,
Foredoomed to dogs and vultures,
    That gallant army came ;
**165** From Setia's purple vineyards,
    From Norba's ancient wall,
From the white streets of Tusculum,
    The proudest town of all ;
From where the Witch's Fortress
**170**    O'erhangs the dark-blue seas ;
From the still glassy lake that sleeps
    Beneath Aricia's trees, —
Those trees in whose dim shadow
    The ghastly priest doth reign,

165. *Setia,* modern *Sezze.*
166. *Norba,* modern *Norma.*
169. The *Witch's Fortress* was *Circeii,* so called because it was the supposed home of Circe.

175 The priest who slew the slayer,
      And shall himself be slain;
   From the drear banks of Ufens,
      Where flights of marsh-fowl play,
   And buffaloes lie wallowing
180    Through the hot summer's day;
   From the gigantic watch-towers,
      No work of earthly men,
   Whence Cora's sentinels o'erlook
      The never-ending fen;
185 From the Laurentian jungle,
      The wild hog's reedy home;
   From the green steeps whence Anio leaps
      In floods of snow-white foam.


11

   Aricia, Cora, Norba,
190    Velitræ, with the might
   Of Setia and of Tusculum,
      Were marshalled on the right:
   The leader was Mamilius,
      Prince of the Latian name;
195 Upon his head a helmet
      Of red gold shone like flame;
   High on a gallant charger

---

175. " According to the story told by Pausanias, Hippolytus, the son of
Theseus, on being raised from the dead by Æsculapius, crossed the sea and
came to Aricia, where he dedicated a temple to Artemis.  The priest of this
temple was to be a runaway slave who had conquered his opponent in single
combat.  Thus a slave who challenged the existing priest and slew him would
himself at once become the priest, and remain so till he should himself be
worsted by another." — Cox.

177. The *Ufens* reappears in modern Italy in *Uffento*, on the banks of the
Poutatore.

183. *Cora*, now *Cori.*

Of dark-gray hue he rode ;
Over his gilded armor
200   A vest of purple flowed,
Woven in the land of sunrise
  By Syria's dark-browed daughters,
And by the sails of Carthage brought
  Far o'er the southern waters.

### 12

205 Lavinium and Laurentum
  Had on the left their post,
With all the banners of the marsh,
  And banners of the coast.
Their leader was false Sextus,
210   That wrought the deed of shame :
With restless pace and haggard face
  To his last field he came.
Man said he saw strange visions
  Which none beside might see,
215 And that strange sounds were in his ears
  Which none might hear but he.
A woman fair and stately,
  But pale as are the dead,
Oft through the watches of the night
220   Sat spinning by his bed.
And as she plied the distaff,
  In a sweet voice and low,
She sang of great old houses,
  And fights fought long ago.
225 So spun she, and so sang she,
  Until the east was gray.

209. See the lay of Horatius, stanza 24.

Then pointed to her bleeding breast,
And shrieked, and fled away.

### 13

But in the centre thickest
230  Were ranged the shields of foes,
And from the centre loudest
The cry of battle rose.
There Tibur marched and Pedum
Beneath proud Tarquin's rule,
235 And Ferentinum of the rock,
And Gabii of the pool.
There rode the Volscian succors:
There, in a dark stern ring,
The Roman exiles gathered close
240  Around the ancient king.
Though white as Mount Soracte,
When winter nights are long,
His beard flowed down o'er mail and belt,
His heart and hand were strong;
245 Under his hoary eyebrows
Still flashed forth quenchless rage,
And, if the lance shook in his gripe,
'T was more with hate than age.
Close at his side was Titus
250  On an Apulian steed,
Titus, the youngest Tarquin,
Too good for such a breed.

### 14

Now on each side the leaders
Gave signal for the charge:
255 And on each side the footmen

Strode on with lance and targe;
And on each side the horsemen
    Struck their spurs deep in gore,
And front to front the armies
260    Met with a mighty roar:
And under that great battle
    The earth with blood was red;
And, like the Pomptine fog at morn,
    The dust hung overhead;
265 And louder still and louder
    Rose from the darkened field
The braying of the war-horns,
    The clang of sword and shield,
The rush of squadrons sweeping
270    Like whirlwinds o'er the plain,
The shouting of the slayers,
    And screeching of the slain.

## 15

False Sextus rode out foremost;
    His look was high and bold;
275 His corselet was of bison's hide,
    Plated with steel and gold.
As glares the famished eagle
    From the Digentian rock
On a choice lamb that bounds alone
280    Before Bandusia's flock,
Herminius glared on Sextus,
    And came with eagle speed,
Herminius on black Auster,
    Brave champion on brave steed;

263. The *Pomptine*, usually called the Pontine, marshes extended over the lowlands of Latium.

285 In his right hand the broadsword
    That kept the bridge so well,
And on his helm the crown he won
    When proud Fidenæ fell.
Woe to the maid whose lover
290    Shall cross his path to-day !
False Sextus saw, and trembled,
    And turned, and fled away.
As turns, as flies, the woodman
    In the Calabrian brake,
295 When through the reeds gleams the round eye
    Of that fell speckled snake ;
So turned, so fled, false Sextus,
    And hid him in the rear,
Behind the dark Lavinian ranks,
300    Bristling with crest and spear.

## 16

But far to north Æbutius,
    The Master of the Knights,
Gave Tubero of Norba
    To feed the Porcian kites.
305 Next under those red horse-hoofs
    Flaccus of Setia lay ;
Better had he been pruning
    Among his elms that day.
Mamilius saw the slaughter,
310    And tossed his golden crest,
And towards the Master of the Knights
    Through the thick battle pressed.
Æbutius smote Mamilius
    So fiercely on the shield
315 That the great lord of Tusculum

    Wellnigh rolled on the field.
Mamilius smote Æbutius,
    With a good aim and true,
Just where the neck and shoulder join,
320    And pierced him through and through;
And brave Æbutius Elva
    Fell swooning to the ground,
But a thick wall of bucklers
    Encompassed him around.
325 His clients from the battle
    Bare him some little space,
And filled a helm from the dark lake,
    And bathed his brow and face;
And when at last he opened
330    His swimming eyes to light,
Men say, the earliest word he spake
    Was, "Friends, how goes the fight?"

### 17

But meanwhile in the centre
    Great deeds of arms were wrought;
335 There Aulus the Dictator
    And there Valerius fought.
Aulus with his good broadsword
    A bloody passage cleared
To where, amidst the thickest foes,
340    He saw the long white beard.
Flat lighted that good broadsword
    Upon proud Tarquin's head.
He dropped the lance; he dropped the reins;

---

325. The word *clients* now applies mainly to those whom lawyers defend in the courts. The Roman term applied to those who were attached to the great Patrician families, and were in turn defended by them.

He fell as fall the dead.
345 Down Aulus springs to slay him,
    With eyes like coals of fire;
But faster Titus hath sprung down,
    And hath bestrode his sire.
Latian captains, Roman knights,
350    Fast down to earth they spring,
And hand to hand they fight on foot
    Around the ancient king.
First Titus gave tall Cæso
    A death wound in the face;
355 Tall Cæso was the bravest man
    Of the brave Fabian race:
Aulus slew Rex of Gabii,
    The priest of Juno's shrine:
Valerius smote down Julius,
360    Of Rome's great Julian line;
Julius, who left his mansion
    High on the Velian hill,
And through all turns of weal and woe
    Followed proud Tarquin still.
365 Now right across proud Tarquin
    A corpse was Julius laid;
And Titus groaned with rage and grief,
    And at Valerius made.
Valerius struck at Titus,
370    And lopped off half his crest;
But Titus stabbed Valerius
    A span deep in the breast.
Like a mast snapped by the tempest,
    Valerius reeled and fell.

---

360. The *Julian* house of Rome professed to trace its lineage back to
Iulus, grandson of Æneas, the Trojan refugee.

375 Ah! woe is me for the good house
    That loves the people well!
Then shouted loud the Latines,
    And with one rush they bore
The struggling Romans backward
380    Three lances' length and more;
And up they took proud Tarquin,
    And laid him on a shield,
And four strong yeomen bare him,
    Still senseless, from the field.

## 18

385 But fiercer grew the fighting
    Around Valerius dead;
For Titus dragged him by the foot,
    And Aulus by the head.
"On, Latines, on!" quoth Titus,
390    "See how the rebels fly!"
"Romans, stand firm!" quoth Aulus,
    "And win this fight or die!
They must not give Valerius
    To raven and to kite;
395 For aye Valerius loathed the wrong,
    And aye upheld the right;
And for your wives and babies
    In the front rank he fell.
Now play the men for the good house
400    That loves the people well!"

## 19

Then tenfold round the body
    The roar of battle rose,
Like the roar of a burning forest

When a strong north-wind blows.
495 Now backward, and now forward,
    Rocked furiously the fray,
Till none could see Valerius,
    And none wist where he lay.
For shivered arms and ensigns
410     Were heaped there in a mound,
And corpses stiff, and dying men
    That writhed and gnawed the ground;
And wounded horses kicking,
    And snorting purple foam;
415 Right well did such a couch befit
    A Consular of Rome.


20

But north looked the Dictator;
    North looked he long and hard;
And spake to Caius Cossus,
420     The Captain of his Guard:
" Caius, of all the Romans
    Thou hast the keenest sight;
Say, what through yonder storm of **dust**
    Comes from the Latian right ? "


21

425 Then answered Caius Cossus:
    " I see an evil sight:
The banner of proud Tusculum
    Comes from the Latian right;
I see the plumed horsemen;
430     And far before the rest
I see the dark-gray charger,
    I see the purple vest;

I see the golden helmet
  That shines far off like flame ;
435 So ever rides Mamilius,
  Prince of the Latian name."


## 22

"Now hearken, Caius Cossus :
  Spring on thy horse's back ;
Ride as the wolves of Apennine
440   Were all upon thy track ;
Haste to our southward battle,
  And never draw thy rein
Until thou find Herminius,
  And bid him come amain."


## 23

445 So Aulus spake, and turned him
  Again to that fierce strife ;
And Caius Cossus mounted,
  And rode for death and life.
Loud clanged beneath his horse-hoofs
450   The helmets of the dead,
And many a curdling pool of blood
  Splashed him from heel to head.
So came he far to southward,
  Where fought the Roman host,
455 Against the banners of the marsh
  And banners of the coast.
Like corn before the sickle
  The stout Lavinians fell,
Beneath the edge of the true sword
460   That kept the bridge so well.

### 24

"Herminius! Aulus greets thee;
   He bids thee come with speed,
To help our central battle;
   For sore is there our need.
465 There wars the youngest Tarquin,
     And there the Crest of Flame,
The Tusculan Mamilius,
     Prince of the Latian name.
Valerius hath fallen fighting
470    In front of our array,
And Aulus of the seventy fields
   Alone upholds the day."

### 25

Herminius beat his bosom,
   But never a word he spake.
475 He clapped his hand on Auster's mane,
   He gave the reins a shake,
Away, away went Auster,
   Like an arrow from the bow;
Black Auster was the fleetest steed
480    From Aufidus to Po.

### 26

Right glad were all the Romans
   Who, in that hour of dread,
Against great odds bare up the war
   Around Valerius dead,

---

466. That is, the gleaming crest on the helmet of the Latin chief.
480. *From Aufidus to Po*, the two rivers which on the south and north
enclose central Italy.

485 When from the south the cheering
    Rose with a mighty swell:
"Herminius comes, Herminius,
    Who kept the bridge so well!"

### 27

Mamilius spied Herminius,
490    And dashed across the way.
"Herminius! I have sought thee
    Through many a bloody day.
One of us two, Herminius,
    Shall nevermore go home.
495 I will lay on for Tusculum,
    And lay thou on for Rome!"

### 28

All round them paused the battle,
    While met in mortal fray
The Roman and the Tusculan,
500    The horses black and gray.
Herminius smote Mamilius
    Through breastplate and through breast;
And fast flowed out the purple blood
    Over the purple vest.
505 Mamilius smote Herminius
    Through head-piece and through head;
And side by side those chiefs of pride
    Together fell down dead.
Down fell they dead together
510    In a great lake of gore;
And still stood all who saw them fall
    While men might count a score.

### 29

Fast, fast, with heels wild spurning,
　　The dark-gray charger fled;
515　He burst through ranks of fighting men,
　　He sprang o'er heaps of dead.
His bridle far out-streaming,
　　His flanks all blood and foam,
He sought the southern mountains,
520　　The mountains of his home.
The pass was steep and rugged,
　　The wolves they howled and whined;
But he ran like a whirlwind up the pass,
　　And he left the wolves behind.
525　Through many a startled hamlet
　　Thundered his flying feet;
He rushed through the gate of Tusculum,
　　He rushed up the long white street;
He rushed by tower and temple,
530　　And paused not from his race
Till he stood before his master's door
　　In the stately market-place.
And straightway round him gathered
　　A pale and trembling crowd,
535 And when they knew him, cries of rage
　　Brake forth, and wailing loud:
And women rent their tresses
　　For their great prince's fall;
And old men girt on their old swords,
540　　And went to man the wall.

### 30

But, like a graven image,
　　Black Auster kept his place,

And ever wistfully he looked
Into his master's face.
545 The raven-mane that daily,
With pats and fond caresses,
The young Herminia washed and combed,
And twined in even tresses,
And decked with colored ribands
550 From her own gay attire,
Hung sadly o'er her father's corpse
In carnage and in mire.

Forth with a shout sprang Titus,
And seized black Auster's rein.
555 Then Aulus sware a fearful oath,
And ran at him amain.
"The furies of thy brother
With me and mine abide,
If one of your accursed house
560 Upon black Auster ride!"
As on an Alpine watch-tower
From heaven comes down the flame,
Full on the neck of Titus
The blade of Aulus came;
565 And out the red blood spouted,
In a wide arch and tall,
As spouts a fountain in the court
Of some rich Capuan's hall.
The knees of all the Latines
570 Were loosened with dismay
When dead, on dead Herminius,
The bravest Tarquin lay.

568. The luxury of Capua has passed into a proverb, since, a hundred
years after this lay was supposed to be sung, Hannibal's soldiers, who could
triumph in battle, were subjugated by Capua's seductions.

### 31

And Aulus the Dictator
    Stroked Auster's raven mane,
575 With heed he looked unto the girths,
    With heed unto the rein.
" Now bear me well, black Auster,
    Into yon thick array;
And thou and I will have revenge
580     For thy good lord this day."

### 32

So spake he ; and was buckling
    Tighter black Auster's band,
When he was aware of a princely pair
    That rode at his right hand.
585 So like they were, no mortal
    Might one from other know;
White as snow their armor was,
    Their steeds were white as snow.
Never on earthly anvil
590     Did such rare armor gleam;
And never did such gallant steeds
    Drink of an earthly stream.

### 33

And all who saw them trembled,
    And pale grew every cheek;
595 And Aulus the Dictator
    Scarce gathered voice to speak.
" Say by what name men call you?
    What city is your home?
And wherefore ride ye in such guise
600     Before the ranks of Rome?"

### 34

"By many names men call us;
  In many lands we dwell:
Well Samothracia knows us;
  Cyrene knows us well.
605 Our house in gay Tarentum
  Is hung each morn with flowers;
High o'er the masts of Syracuse
  Our marble portal towers;
But by the proud Eurotas
610   Is our dear native home;
And for the right we come to fight
  Before the ranks of Rome."

### 35

So answered those strange horsemen,
  And each couched low his spear;
615 And forthwith all the ranks of Rome
  Were bold, and of good cheer.
And on the thirty armies
  Came wonder and affright,
And Ardea wavered on the left,
620   And Cora on the right.
"Rome to the charge!" cried Aulus;
  "The foe begins to yield!
Charge for the hearth of Vesta!
  Charge for the Golden Shield!
625 Let no man stop to plunder,

---

603. *Samothracia* was an island in the Ægean.
604. *Cyrene* was a Greek colony on the north coast of Africa.
605. *Tarentum*, a wealthy Greek city in southern Italy.
609. The *Eurotas* was the river flowing past Lacedæmon.
624. The *Golden Shield*, in the traditions of Rome, was that of the god Mars,
which had fallen from heaven in the days of Numa Pompilius.

But slay, and slay, and slay;
The gods who live forever
Are on our side to-day."

### 36

Then the fierce trumpet-flourish
630    From earth to heaven arose.
The kites know well the long stern **swell**
That bids the Romans close.
Then the good sword of Aulus
Was lifted up to slay;
635 Then, like a crag down Apennine,
Rushed Auster through the **fray.**
But under those strange horsemen
Still thicker lay the slain;
And after those strange horses
640    Black Auster toiled in vain.
Behind them Rome's long battle
Came rolling on the foe,
Ensigns dancing wild above,
Blades all in line below.
645 So comes the Po in flood-time
Upon the Celtic plain;
So comes the squall, blacker than **night,**
Upon the Adrian main.
Now, by our Sire Quirinus,
650    It was a goodly sight
To see the thirty standards
Swept down the tide of flight.
So flies the spray of Adria
When the black squall doth blow,
655 So corn-sheaves in the flood-time

649. *Quirinus* was the name of the deified Romulus.

Spin down the whirling.Po.
False Sextus to the mountains
    Turned first his horse's head;
And fast fled Ferentinum,
560    And fast Lanuvium fled.
The horsemen of Nomentum
    Spurred hard out of the fray;
The footmen of Velitræ
    Threw shield and spear away.
565 And underfoot was trampled,
    Amidst the mud and gore,
The banner of proud Tusculum,
    That never stooped before.
And down went Flavius Faustus,
570    Who led his stately ranks
From where the apple-blossoms wave
    On Anio's echoing banks,
And Tullus of Arpinum,
    Chief of the Volscian aids,
575 And Metius with the long fair curls,
    The love of Anxur's maids,
And the white head of Vulso,
    The great Arician seer,
And Nepos of Laurentum,
580    The hunter of the deer;
And in the back false Sextus
    Felt the good Roman steel,
And wriggling in the dust he died,
    Like a worm beneath the wheel.
585 And fliers and pursuers
    Were mingled in a mass,
And far away the battle
    Went roaring through the pass.

37

Sempronius Atratinus
690    Sate in the Eastern Gate,
     Beside him were three Fathers,
       Each in his chair of state ;
   Fabius, whose nine stout grandsons
     That day were in the field,
695 And Manlius, eldest of the Twelve
     Who kept the Golden Shield ;
   And Sergius, the High Pontiff,
     For wisdom far renowned ;
   In all Etruria's colleges
700    Was no such Pontiff found.
   And all around the portal,
     And high above the wall,
   Stood a great throng of people,
     But sad and silent all ;
705 Young lads, and stooping elders
     That might not bear the mail,
   Matrons with lips that quivered,
     And maids with faces pale.
   Since the first gleam of daylight,
710    Sempronius had not ceased
   To listen for the rushing
     Of horse-hoofs from the east.
   The mist of eve was rising,
     The sun was hastening down,
715 When he was aware of a princely pair
     Fast pricking towards the town.
   So like they were, man never

---

695. The *Twelve* were the Patrician custodians of the Golden Shield and its
eleven imitations, for eleven others were made, it was said, to reduce the
chances of theft.

Saw twins so like before;
Red with gore their armor was,
720    Their steeds were red with gore.

### 38

"Hail to the great Asylum!
Hail to the hill-tops seven!
Hail to the fire that burns for aye,
And the shield that fell from heaven!
725 This day, by Lake Regillus,
Under the Porcian height,
All in the lands of Tusculum
Was fought a glorious fight;
To-morrow your Dictator
730    Shall bring in triumph home
The spoils of thirty cities
To deck the shrines of Rome!"

### 39

Then burst from that great concourse
A shout that shook the towers,
735 And some ran north, and some ran south,
Crying, "The day is ours!"
But on rode these strange horsemen,
With slow and lordly pace;
And none who saw their bearing
740    Durst ask their name or race.
On rode they to the Forum,
While laurel-boughs and flowers,
From house-tops and from windows,
Fell on their crests in showers.

---

721. *The great Asylum*, for Romulus was said to promise a refuge in his new
ity to all fugitives.

745 When they drew nigh to Vesta,
    They vaulted down amain,
And washed their horses in the well
    That springs by Vesta's fane.
And straight again they mounted,
750     And rode to Vesta's door;
Then, like a blast, away they passed,
    And no man saw them more.

### 40

And all the people trembled,
    And pale grew every cheek;
755 And Sergius the High Pontiff
    Alone found voice to speak:
"The gods who live forever
    Have fought for Rome to-day!
These be the Great Twin Brethren
760     To whom the Dorians pray.
Back comes the Chief in triumph
    Who, in the hour of fight,
Hath seen the Great Twin Brethren
    In harness on his right.
765 Safe comes the ship to haven,
    Through billows and through gales,
If once the Great Twin Brethren
    Sit shining on the sails.
Wherefore they washed their horses
770     In Vesta's holy well,
Wherefore they rode to Vesta's door,
    I know, but may not tell.
Here, hard by Vesta's Temple,
    Build we a stately dome

---

760. The *Dorians* were one of the foremost tribes of the Greek race.

TEMPLES OF VESTA AND CASTORES (Auer's Reconstruction)

*From Lanciani's Ruins and Excavations of Ancient Rome*

775 Unto the Great Twin Brethren
 Who fought so well for Rome.
And when the months returning
 Bring back this day of fight,
The proud Ides of Quintilis,
780 Marked evermore with white,
Unto the Great Twin Brethren
 Let all the people throng,
With chaplets and with offerings,
 With music and with song;
785 And let the doors and windows
 Be hung with garlands all,
And let the Knights be summoned
 To Mars without the wall.
Thence let them ride in purple
790 With joyous trumpet-sound,
Each mounted on his war-horse,
 And each with olive crowned;
And pass in solemn order
 Before the sacred dome,
795 Where dwell the Great Twin Brethren
 Who fought so well for Rome!"

# VIRGINIA.

A COLLECTION consisting exclusively of war-songs would give an imperfect, or rather an erroneous, notion of the spirit of the old Latin ballads. The Patricians, during more than a century after the expulsion of the Kings, held all the high military commands. A Plebeian, even though, like Lucius Siccius, he were distinguished by his valor and knowledge of war, could serve only in subordinate posts. A minstrel, therefore, who wished to celebrate the early triumphs of his country, could hardly take any but Patricians for his heroes. The warriors who are mentioned in the two preceding lays — Horatius, Lartius, Herminius, Aulus Posthumius, Æbutius Elva, Sempronius Atratinus, Valerius Poplicola — were all members of the dominant order; and a poet who was singing their praises, whatever his own political opinions might be, would naturally abstain from insulting the class to which they belonged, and from reflecting on the system which had placed such men at the head of the legions of the Commonwealth.

But there was a class of compositions in which the great families were by no means so courteously treated. No parts of early Roman history are richer with poetical coloring than those which relate to the long contest between the privileged houses and the commonalty. The population of Rome was, from a very early period, divided into hereditary castes, which, indeed, readily united to repel foreign enemies, but which regarded each other, during many years, with bitter animosity. . . . Among the grievances under which the Plebeians suffered three were felt as peculiarly severe. They were excluded from the highest magistracies; they were excluded from all share in the public lands; and they were ground down to the dust by partial and barbarous legislation touching pecuniary contracts. The ruling class in Rome was a moneyed class; and it made and administered the laws with a view solely to its own interest. Thus the relation between lender and borrower was mixed up with the relation between sovereign and subject. The great men held a large portion of the community in dependence by means of advances at enormous usury. The law of debt, framed by creditors and for the protection of creditors, was the most horrible that has ever been known among men. The liberty, and even the life, of the insolvent were at the mercy of the Patrician money-lenders. Children often became slaves in consequence of the misfortunes of their parents. The debtor was imprisoned, not in a public gaol under the care of impartial public functionaries, but in a private workhouse belonging to the creditor. Frightful stories were told respecting these dungeons. It was said that torture and brutal violation were common; that tight stocks, heavy chains, scanty measures of food, were used to punish wretches guilty of nothing but poverty; and that brave soldiers, whose breasts were covered with honorable scars, were often marked still more deeply on the back by the scourges of high-born usurers.

The Plebeians were, however, not wholly without constitutional rights. From an early period they had been admitted to some share of political power. They were enrolled each in his century, and were allowed a share, considerable though not proportioned to their numerical strength, in the disposal of those high dignities from which they were themselves excluded. . . . The Plebeians had also the privilege of annually appointing officers, named Tribunes, who had no active share in the government of the Commonwealth, but who, by degrees, acquired a power formidable even to the ablest and most resolute Consuls and Dictators. The person of the Tribune was inviolable ; and, though he could directly effect little, he could obstruct everything.

During more than a century after the institution of the Tribuneship, the Commons struggled manfully for the removal of grievances under which they labored ; and, in spite of many checks and reverses, succeeded in wringing concession after concession from the stubborn aristocracy. At length, in the year of the city 378, both parties mustered their whole strength for their last and most desperate conflict. The popular and active Tribune, Caius Licinius, proposed the three memorable laws which are called by his name, and which were intended to redress the three great evils of which the Plebeians complained. He was supported with eminent ability and firmness by his colleague, Lucius Sextius. The struggle appears to have been the fiercest that ever in any community terminated without an appeal to arms. If such a contest had raged in any Greek city, the streets would have run with blood. But, even in the paroxysms of faction, the Roman retained his gravity, his respect for law, and his tenderness for the lives of his fellow-citizens. Year after year, Licinius and Sextius were reëlected Tribunes. Year after year, if the narrative which has come down to us is to be trusted, they continued to exert to the full extent their power of stopping the whole machine of government. No curule magistrates could be chosen; no military muster could be held. We know too little of the state of Rome in those days to be able to conjecture how, during that long anarchy, the peace was kept and ordinary justice administered between man and man. The animosity of both parties rose to the greatest height. The excitement, we may well suppose, would have been particularly intense at the annual election of the Tribunes. On such occasions there can be little doubt that the great families did all that could be done, by threats and caresses, to break the union of the Plebeians. That union, however, proved indissoluble. At length the good cause triumphed. The Licinian laws were carried. Lucius Sextius was the first Plebeian Consul, Caius Licinius the third.

The results of this great change were singularly happy and glorious. Two centuries of prosperity, harmony, and victory followed the reconciliation of the orders. Men who remembered Rome engaged in waging petty wars almost within sight of the Capitol lived to see her the mistress of Italy. While the disabilities of the Plebeians continued, she was hardly able to maintain her ground against the Volscians and Hernicans. When those disabilities were removed, she rapidly became more than a match for Carthage and Macedon.

During the great Licinian contest the Plebeian poets were, doubtless, not silent. . . . These minstrels, as Niebuhr has remarked, appear to have generally taken the popular side. We can hardly be mistaken in supposing that, at the great crisis of the civil conflict, they employed themselves in versifying all the most powerful and virulent speeches of the Tribunes, and in heaping abuse on the leaders of the aristocracy. Every personal defect, every domestic scandal, every tradition dishonorable to a noble house, would be sought out, brought into notice, and exaggerated. The illustrious head of the aristocratical party, Marcus Furius Camillus, might perhaps be, in some measure, protected by his venerable age, and by the memory of his great services to the state. But Appius Claudius Crassus enjoyed no such immunity. He was descended from a long line of ancestors distinguished by their haughty demeanor, and by the inflexibility with which they had withstood all the demands of the Plebeian order. While the political conduct and the deportment of the Claudian nobles drew upon them the fiercest public hatred, they were accused of wanting, if any credit is due to the early history of Rome, a class of qualities which, in the military commonwealth, is sufficient to cover a multitude of offences. The chief of the family appear to have been eloquent, versed in civil business, and learned after the fashion of their age ; but in war they were not distinguished by skill or valor. Some of them, as if conscious where their weakness lay, had, when filling the highest magistracies, taken internal administration as their department of public business, and left the military command to their colleagues. One of them had been intrusted with an army, and had failed ignominiously. None of them had been honored with a triumph. None of them had achieved any martial exploit, such as those by which Lucius Quinctius Cincinnatus, Titus Quinctius Capitolinus, Aulus Cornelius Cossus, and, above all, the great Camillus, had extorted

the reluctant esteem of the multitude. During the Licin-
ian conflict, Appius Claudius Crassus signalized himself
by the ability and severity with which he harangued
against the two great agitators. He would naturally,
therefore, be the favorite mark of the Plebeian sat-
irists ; nor would they have been at a loss to find a point
on which he was open to attack.

His grandfather, called, like himself, Appius Clau-
dius, had left a name as much detested as that of Sextus
Tarquinius. He had been Consul more than seventy
years before the introduction of the Licinian laws. By
availing himself of a singular crisis in public feeling, he
had obtained the consent of the Commons to the aboli-
tion of the Tribuneship, and had been chief of that
Council of Ten to which the whole direction of the
state had been committed. In a few months his admin-
istration had become universally odious. It was swept
away by an irresistible outbreak of popular fury, and its
memory was still held in abhorrence by the whole city.
The immediate cause of the downfall of this execrable
government was said to have been an attempt made by
Appius Claudius to get possession of a beautiful young
girl of humble birth. The story ran that the Decemvir,
unable to succeed by bribes and solicitations, resorted to
an outrageous act of tyranny. A vile dependent of
the Claudian house laid claim to the damsel as his slave.
The cause was brought before the tribunal of Appius.
The wicked magistrate, in defiance of the clearest
proofs, gave judgment for the claimant. But the girl's
father, a brave soldier, saved her from servitude and
dishonor by stabbing her to the heart in the sight of the
whole Forum. That blow was the signal for a general
explosion. Camp and city rose at once ; the Ten were

pulled down; the Tribuneship was reëstablished; and
Appius escaped the hands of the executioner only by a
voluntary death.

It can hardly be doubted that a story so admirably
adapted to the purposes both of the poet and of the
demagogue would be eagerly seized upon by minstrels
burning with hatred against the Patrician order, against
the Claudian house, and especially against the grandson
and namesake of the infamous Decemvir.

In order that the reader may judge fairly of these
fragments of the lay of Virginia, he must imagine him-
self a Plebeian who has just voted for the reëlection of
Sextius and Licinius. All the power of the Patricians
has been exerted to throw out the two great champions
of the Commons. Every Posthumius, Æmilius, and
Cornelius has used his influence to the utmost. Debtors
have been let out of the workhouses on condition of
voting against the men of the people; clients have been
posted to hiss and interrupt the favorite candidates;
Appius Claudius Crassus has spoken with more than his
usual eloquence and asperity: all has been in vain;
Licinius and Sextius have a fifth time carried all the
tribes; work is suspended; the booths are closed; the
Plebeians bear on their shoulders the two champions of
liberty through the Forum. Just at this moment it is
announced that a popular poet, a zealous adherent of
the Tribunes, has made a new song which will cut the
Claudian nobles to the heart. The crowd gathers round
him, and calls on him to recite it. He takes his stand
on the spot where, according to tradition, Virginia,
more than seventy years ago, was seized by the pander
of Appius, and begins his story.

[Macaulay calls this lay "fragments of a lay," and

the . . . which indicate breaks in the story are his, and
not the editor's. The poem is given just as Macaulay
wrote it.]

## VIRGINIA.

FRAGMENTS OF A LAY SUNG IN THE FORUM ON THE
DAY WHEREON LUCIUS SEXTIUS SEXTINUS LATERANUS
AND CAIUS LICINIUS CALVUS STOLO WERE ELECTED
TRIBUNES OF THE COMMONS THE FIFTH TIME, IN
THE YEAR OF THE CITY CCCLXXXII.

YE good men of the Commons, with loving hearts
    and true,
Who stand by the bold Tribunes that still have
    stood by you,
Come, make a circle round me, and mark my tale
    with care,
A tale of what Rome once hath borne, of what
    Rome yet may bear.
5 This is no Grecian fable, of fountains running
    wine,
Of maids with snaky tresses, or sailors turned to
    swine.
Here, in this very Forum, under the noonday sun,
In sight of all the people, the bloody deed was
    done.

---

5. One of the Homeric hymns sings of a purple stream of wine running
along the decks of a ship on which the god Bacchus was confined.

6. See the fable of the Gorgons and the Homeric tale of Circe's enchant-
ment.

Old men still creep among us who saw that fearful
day,

10 Just seventy years and seven ago, when the wicked
Ten bare sway.


Of all the wicked Ten still the names are held
accursed,

And of all the wicked Ten Appius Claudius was
the worst.

He stalked along the Forum like King Tarquin in
his pride ;

Twelve axes waited on him, six marching on a
side ;

15 The townsmen shrank to right and left, and eyed
askance with fear

His lowering brow, his curling mouth, which always
seemed to sneer :

That brow of hate, that mouth of scorn, marks all
the kindred still ;

For never was there Claudius yet but wished the
Commons ill ;

Nor lacks he fit attendance ; for close behind his
heels,

20 With outstretched chin and crouching pace, the
client Marcus steals,

His loins girt up to run with speed, be the errand
what it may,

And the smile flickering on his cheek, for aught his
lord may say.


10. The decemvirs, when first appointed to draw up a new code of laws and
to perform the duties of magistrates, were acceptable to the people, but
when firmly seated in power became tyrannical.

18. The *Commons.* By this familiar English term Macaulay renders the
Latin *plebs.*

Such varlets pimp and jest for hire among the lying
    Greeks:

Such varlets still are paid to hoot when brave Li-
    cinius speaks.

25 Where'er ye shed the honey, the buzzing flies will
    crowd ;

Where'er ye fling the carrion, the raven's croak
    is loud ;

Where'er down Tiber garbage floats, the greedy
    pike ye see ;

And wheresoe'er such lord is found, such client
    still will be.

Just then, as through one cloudless chink in a
    black stormy sky,

30 Shines out the dewy morning - star, a fair young
    girl came by.

With her small tablets in her hand, and her satchel
    on her arm,

Home she went bounding from the school, nor
    dreamed of shame or harm ;

And past those dreaded axes she innocently ran,

With bright, frank brow that had not learned to
    blush at gaze of man ;

35 And up the Sacred Street she turned, and, as she
    danced along,

She warbled gayly to herself lines of the good old
    song,

How for a sport the princes came spurring from
    the camp,

24. *Licinius* was one of the first Tribunes of the people.

31. The *tablets* were wax tablets, and served the same purpose as slates now-
adays.

35. The *Sacred Street* was the *Via Sacra* leading to the Forum.

And found Lucrece, combing the fleece, under the
    midnight lamp.

The maiden sang as sings the lark, when up he
    darts his flight,

40 From his nest in the green April corn, to meet the
    morning light ;

And Appius heard her sweet young voice, and saw
    her sweet young face,

And loved her with the accursed love of his ac-
    cursed race,

And all along the Forum, and up the Sacred
    Street,

His vulture eye pursued the trip of those small
    glancing feet.

   .    .    .    .    .    .    .    .    .

45    Over the Alban mountains the light of morning
    broke ;

From all the roofs of the Seven Hills curled the
    thin wreaths of smoke.

The city-gates were opened ; the Forum all alive,

With buyers and with sellers was humming like a
    hive.

Blithely on brass and timber the craftsman's stroke
    was ringing,

50 And blithely o'er her panniers the market-girl was
    singing,

And blithely young Virginia came smiling from her
    home :

38. There had been a wager among the princes of Rome, when round their
camp-fire outside of the city, as to which of their wives was most loyal, and they
rode into the city at midnight to find all engaged in feasting save Lucrece, who
was spinning in the midst of her maids.

THE ROMAN FORUM

Ah! woe for young Virginia, the sweetest maid in
Rome!

With her small tablets in her hand, and her satchel
on her arm,

Forth she went bounding to the school, nor dreamed
of shame or harm.

55 She crossed the Forum shining with stalls in alleys
gay,

And just had reached the very spot whereon I
stand this day,

When up the varlet Marcus came; not such as
when erewhile

He crouched behind his patron's heels with the
true client smile:

He came with lowering forehead, swollen features,
and clenched fist,

60 And strode across Virginia's path, and caught her
by the wrist.

Hard strove the frighted maiden, and screamed
with look aghast;

And at her scream from right and left the folk
came running fast;

The money-changer Crispus, with his thin silver
hairs,

And Hanno from the stately booth glittering with
Punic wares,

65 And the strong smith Muræna, grasping a half-
forged brand,

And Volero the flesher, his cleaver in his hand.

All came in wrath and wonder; for all knew that
fair child;

64 *Punic wares,* i. e., merchandise brought from Carthage. *Hanno* itself
is a Carthaginian name.

And, as she passed them twice a day, all kissed
 their hands and smiled ;
And the strong smith Muræna gave Marcus such a
 blow,
70 The caitiff reeled three paces back, and let the
 maiden go.
Yet glared he fiercely round him, and growled in
 harsh, fell tone,
" She 's mine, and I will have her : I seek but for
 mine own :
She is my slave, born in my house, and stolen away
 and sold,
The year of the sore sickness, ere she was twelve
 hours old.
75 'T was in the sad September, the month of wail
 and fright,
Two augurs were borne forth that morn ; the Con-
 sul died ere night.
I wait on Appius Claudius, I waited on his sire ;
Let him who works the client wrong beware the
 patron's ire ! "

So spake the varlet Marcus ; and dread and
 silence came
80 On all the people at the sound of the great Clau-
 dian name.
For then there was no Tribune to speak the word
 of might,
Which makes the rich man tremble, and guards
 the poor man's right.
There was no brave Licinius, no honest Sextius
 then ;

But all the city, in great fear, obeyed the wicked
    Ten.
35 Yet ere the varlet Marcus again might seize the
    maid,
Who clung tight to Muræna's skirt, and sobbed and
    shrieked for aid,
Forth through the throng of gazers the young Icil-
    ius pressed,
And stamped his foot, and rent his gown, and
    smote upon his breast,
And sprang upon that column, by many a minstrel
    sung,
90 Whereon three mouldering helmets, three rusting
    swords, are hung,
And beckoned to the people, and in bold voice and
    clear
Poured thick and fast the burning words which ty-
    rants quake to hear.

"Now, by your children's cradles, now by your
    fathers' graves,
Be men to-day, Quirites, or be forever slaves!
95 For this did Servius give us laws? For this did
    Lucrece bleed?
For this was the great vengeance wrought on Tar-
    quin's evil seed?
For this did those false sons make red the axes of
    their sire?

95. *Servius* was the King Servius Tullius under whose rule the Romans
were organized into a military community.
97. The *false sons* were the two sons of Brutus, one of the consuls elected
after the expulsion of Tarquin. They were beheaded at the order of their
father for conspiring to restore the tyrant.

For this did Scævola's right hand hiss in the Tus-
 can fire ?

Shall the vile fox-earth awe the race that stormed
 the lion's den ?

**100** Shall we, who could not brook one lord, crouch to
 the wicked Ten ?

Oh for that ancient spirit which curbed the Senate's
 will !

Oh for the tents which in old time whitened the
 Sacred Hill !

In those brave days our fathers stood firmly side
 by side ;

They faced the Marcian fury ; they tamed the Fa-
 bian pride ;

**105** They drove the fiercest Quinctius an outcast forth
 from Rome ;

They sent the haughtiest Claudius with shivered
 fasces home.

But what their care bequeathed us our madness
 flung away :

98. Mucius Scævola, bent on murdering Lars Porsena, contrived to get en-
trance to the Tuscan camp. He murdered the wrong man by mistake, and on
being discovered thrust his hand into the fire to show that he cared nothing
for torture, and then declared that he had 300 companions as brave as he.
This display of courage induced the Etruscan chief to make overtures of
peace to the Romans.

102. That is, when the Plebs withdrew from Rome until their demands
were granted and Tribunes appointed.

104. Caius Marcius, a young Patrician, better known as Coriolanus, was
banished from Rome, and taking service with the Volscians reduced his coun-
trymen to extremities.   *The Fabian pride* refers to the action of the troops
of Cæso Fabius when they refused to storm the camp of the enemy, and so,
by leaving the victory incomplete, deprived the general of his triumph.

105. Quinctius Cincinnatus was an opponent of the Plebs, and was banished
by that party.

106. Appius Claudius, head of the Patrician gens of the name, was so harsh
in his treatment of the people that he brought down on himself mob-treat-
ment.

All the ripe fruit of threescore years was blighted
  in a day.

Exult, ye proud Patricians! The hard-fought fight
  is o'er.

110 We strove for honors — 't was in vain; for free-
  dom — 't is no more.

No crier to the polling summons the eager throng;

No Tribune breathes the word of might that guards
  the weak from wrong.

Our very hearts, that were so high, sink down be-
  neath your will.

Riches, and lands, and power, and state — ye have
  them : — keep them still.

115 Still keep the holy fillets; still keep the purple
  gown,

The axes, and the curule chair, the car, and laurel
  crown :

Still press us for your cohorts, and, when the fight
  is done,

Still fill your garners from the soil which our good
  swords have won.

Still, like a spreading ulcer, which leech-craft may
  not cure,

120 Let your foul usance eat away the substance of the
  poor.

115. The *holy fillets* were worn by the priestly class, which was strictly Pa-
trician ; the *purple gown* was worn by the consul and knights on public occa-
sions.

116. The *curule chair* was the chair of state. It is represented often in
modern statuary, as in the statue of Lincoln in Chicago. The consuls used a
*car* or chariot in the triumphal processions after a war, and wore a wreath or
garland of laurel.

117. There were ten *cohorts* in every Roman legion, but the number of men
in a legion varied.

120. One of the greatest grievances of the Plebeians lay in the usury prac-
ticed by the Patricians, and the cruelty of the laws regarding debt.

Still let your haggard debtors bear all their fathers
bore;

Still let your dens of torment be noisome as of
yore;

No fire when Tiber freezes; no air in dogstar
heat;

And store of rods for free-born backs, and holes
for free-born feet.

125 Heap heavier still the fetters; bar closer still the
grate;

Patient as sheep we yield us up unto your cruel
hate.

But, by the Shades beneath us, and by the gods
above,

Add not unto your cruel hate your yet more cruel
love!

Have ye not graceful ladies, whose spotless lineage
springs

130 From Consuls, and High Pontiffs, and ancient Al-
ban kings?

Ladies, who deign not on our paths to set their ten-
der feet,

Who from their cars look down with scorn upon
the wondering street,

Who in Corinthian mirrors their own proud smiles
behold,

And breathe of Capuan odors, and shine with Span-
ish gold?

135 Then leave the poor Plebeian his single tie to
life —

The sweet, sweet love of daughter, of sister, and
of wife,

133. Corinth, in Greece, was famous for its luxurious living.

The gentle speech, the balm for all that his vexed
soul endures,

The kiss, in which he half forgets even such a yoke
as yours.

Still let the maiden's beauty swell the father's
breast with pride ;

140 Still let the bridegroom's arms infold an unpolluted
bride.

Spare us the inexpiable wrong, the unutterable
shame,

That turns the coward's heart to steel, the slug-
gard's blood to flame,

Lest, when our latest hope is fled, ye taste of our
despair,

And learn by proof, in some wild hour, how much
the wretched dare."

. . . . . . . . . .

. . . . . . . . . .

145    Straightway Virginius led the maid a little space
aside,

To where the reeking shambles stood, piled up with
horn and hide,

Close to yon low dark archway, where, in a crim-
son flood,

Leaps down to the great sewer the gurgling stream
of blood.

Hard by, a flesher on a block had laid his whittle
down ;

150 Virginius caught the whittle up, and hid it in his
gown.

And then his eyes grew very dim, and his throat
began to swell,

And in a hoarse, changed voice he spake, " Fare-
well, sweet child !   Farewell !

Oh, how I loved my darling! Though stern I
　　sometimes be,

To thee, thou know'st I was not so. Who could be
　　so to thee ?

155 And how my darling loved me! How glad she
　　was to hear

My footstep on the threshold when I came back
　　last year !

And how she danced with pleasure to see my civic
　　crown,

And took my sword, and hung it up, and brought
　　me forth my gown !

Now all those things are over, — yes, all thy pretty
　　ways,

160 Thy needlework, thy prattle, thy snatches of old
　　lays ;

And none will grieve when I go forth, or smile
　　when I return,

Or watch beside the old man's bed, or weep upon
　　his urn.

The house that was the happiest within the Roman
　　walls,

The house that envied not the wealth of Capua's
　　marble halls,

165 Now, for the brightness of thy smile, must have
　　eternal gloom,

And for the music of thy voice, the silence of the
　　tomb.

The time is come. See how he points his eager
　　hand this way !

---

157. The *civic crown* of oak leaves was conferred on a soldier who had
saved a comrade in battle by killing his opponent.

158. The *gown* or *toga* was the mark of the Roman citizen.

See how his eyes gloat on thy grief, like a kite's
    upon the prey!
With all his wit, he little deems that, spurned, be-
    trayed, bereft,
170 Thy father hath in his despair one fearful refuge
    left.
He little deems that in this hand I clutch what still
    can save
Thy gentle youth from taunts and blows, the por-
    tion of the slave;
Yea, and from nameless evil, that passeth taunt
    and blow, —
Foul outrage which thou knowest not, which thou
    shalt never know.
175 Then clasp me round the neck once more, and give
    me one more kiss;
And now, mine own dear little girl, there is no way
    but this."
With that he lifted high the steel, and smote her in
    the side,
And in her blood she sank to earth, and with one
    sob she died.

Then, for a little moment, all people held their
    breath;
180 And through the crowded Forum was stillness as
    of death;
And in another moment brake forth from one
    and all
A cry as if the Volscians were coming o'er the
    wall.
Some with averted faces shrieking fled home
    amain;

Some ran to call a leech ; and some ran to lift the
    slain ;
135 Some felt her lips and little wrist, if life might
    there be found ;
And some tore up their garments fast, and strove
    to stanch the wound.
In vain they ran, and felt, and stanched, for never
    truer blow
That good right arm had dealt in fight against a
    Volscian foe.

When Appius Claudius saw that deed, he shud-
    dered and sank down,
190 And hid his face some little space with the corner
    of his gown,
Till, with white lips and bloodshot eyes, Virginius
    tottered nigh,
And stood before the judgment-seat, and held the
    knife on high.
" O dwellers in the nether gloom, avengers of the
    slain,
By this dear blood I cry to you, do right between
    us twain ;
195 And even as Appius Claudius hath dealt by me
    and mine,
Deal you by Appius Claudius and all the Claudian
    line ! "
So spake the slayer of his child, and turned, and
    went his way ;
But first he cast one haggard glance to where the
    body lay,
And writhed, and groaned a fearful groan, and
    then, with steadfast feet,

**200** Strode right across the market-place unto the Sacred Street.

Then up sprang Appius Claudius: "Stop him, alive or dead!
Ten thousand pounds of copper to the man who brings his head!"
He looked upon his clients; but none would work his will.
He looked upon his lictors; but they trembled and stood still.
**205** And, as Virginius through the press his way in silence cleft,
Ever the mighty multitude fell back to right and left.
And he hath passed in safety unto his woful home,
And there ta'en horse to tell the camp what deeds are done in Rome.

By this the flood of people was swollen from every side,
**210** And streets and porches round were filled with that o'erflowing tide;
And close around the body gathered a little train
Of them that were the nearest and dearest to the slain.
They brought a bier, and hung it with many a cypress crown,
And gently they uplifted her, and gently laid her down.
**215** The face of Appius Claudius wore the Claudian scowl and sneer,

And in the Claudian note he cried, "What doth
    this rabble here ?
Have they no crafts to mind at home, that hither-
    ward they stray ?
Ho ! lictors, clear the market-place, and fetch the
    corpse away ! "
The voice of grief and fury till then had not been
    loud ;
220 But a deep sullen murmur wandered among the
    crowd,
Like the moaning noise that goes before the whirl-
    wind on the deep,
Or the growl of a fierce watch-dog but half aroused
    from sleep.
But when the lictors at that word, all yeomen all
    and strong,
Each with his axe and sheaf of twigs, went down
    into the throng,
225 Those old men say, who saw that day of sorrow
    and of sin,
That in the Roman Forum was never such a din.
The wailing, hooting, cursing, the howls of grief
    and hate,
Were heard beyond the Pincian Hill, beyond the
    Latin Gate.
But close around the body, where stood the little train
230 Of them that were the nearest and dearest to the
    slain,
No cries were there, but teeth set fast, low whis-
    pers and black frowns,
And breaking up of benches, and girding up of
    gowns ;
'T was well the lictors might not pierce to where
    the maiden lay,

Else surely had they been all twelve torn limb from
 limb that day.

**235** Right glad they were to struggle back, blood stream-
 ing from their heads,

With axes all in splinters, and raiment all in
 shreds.

Then Appius Claudius gnawed his lip and the
 blood left his cheek;

And thrice he beckoned with his hand, and thrice
 he strove to speak;

And thrice the tossing Forum set up a frightful
 yell:

**240** "See, see, thou dog! what thou hast done; and
 hide thy shame in hell!

Thou that wouldst make our maidens slaves must
 first make slaves of men.

Tribunes! Hurrah for Tribunes! Down with the
 wicked Ten!"

And straightway, thick as hailstones, came whiz-
 zing through the air

Pebbles, and bricks, and potsherds, all round the
 curule chair;

**245** And upon Appius Claudius great fear and trem-
 bling came;

For never was a Claudius yet brave against aught
 but shame.

Though the great houses love us not, we own, to do
 them right,

That the great houses, all save one, have borne
 them well in fight.

Still Caius of Corioli, his triumphs and his wrongs,

249. *Caius of Corioli.* Coriolanus took his name from the town he had
conquered. See note to line 104.

250 His vengeance and his mercy, live in our camp-fire
     songs.

Beneath the yoke of Furius oft have Gaul and
     Tuscan bowed;

And Rome may bear the pride of him of whom
     herself is proud.

But evermore a Claudius shrinks from a stricken
     field,

And changes color like a maid at sight of sword
     and shield.

255 The Claudian triumphs all were won within the
     city towers;

The Claudian yoke was never pressed on any necks
     but ours.

A Cossus, like a wild-cat, springs ever at the
     face;

A Fabius rushes like a boar against the shouting
     chase;

But the vile Claudian litter, raging with currish
     spite,

260 Still yelps and snaps at those who run, still runs
     from those who smite.

So now 't was seen of Appius. When stones be-
     gan to fly,

He shook, and crouched, and wrung his hands, and
     smote upon his thigh.

"Kind clients, honest lictors, stand by me in this
     fray!

Must I be torn in pieces? Home, home, the near-
     est way!"

251. Marcus Furius Camillus of Tusculum delivered Rome from the Gauls.
257. *Cossus* was the surname of a house belonging to the gens Cornelia.
258. The Fabian gens was noted for its bravery.

265 While yet he spake, and looked around with a be-
    wildered stare,
    Four sturdy lictors put their necks beneath the
    curule chair;
    And fourscore clients on the left, and fourscore on
    the right,
    Arrayed themselves with swords and staves, and
    loins girt up for fight.
    But, though without or staff or sword, so furious
    was the throng,
270 That scarce the train with might and main could
    bring their lord along.
    Twelve times the crowd made at him; five times
    they seized his gown;
    Small chance was his to rise again, if once they got
    him down.
    And sharper came the pelting; and evermore the
    yell —
    " Tribunes ! we will have Tribunes ! " rose with a
    louder swell.
275 And the chair tossed as tosses a bark with tat-
    tered sail
    When raves the Adriatic beneath an eastern gale,
    When the Calabrian sea-marks are lost in clouds of
    spume,
    And the great Thunder Cape has donned his veil of
    inky gloom.
    One stone hit Appius in the mouth, and one beneath
    the ear;
280 And ere he reached Mount Palatine, he swooned
    with pain and fear.

278. The *Thunder Cape* was a region of volcanic fire on the eastern
coast of the Adriatic, facing the modern Brindisi.

His cursed head, that he was wont to hold so high
    with pride,
Now, like a drunken man's, hung down, and swayed
    from side to side ;
And when his stout retainers had brought him to
    his door,
His face and neck were all one cake of filth and
    clotted gore.
285 As Appius Claudius was that day, so may his
    grandson be !
God send Rome one such other sight, and send me
    there to see !

. . . . . . . . . . . .

# THE PROPHECY OF CAPYS.

IT can hardly be necessary to remind any reader that, according to the popular tradition, Romulus, after he had slain his grand-uncle, Amulius, and restored his grandfather Numitor, determined to quit Alba, the hereditary domain of the Sylvian princes, and to found a new city. The gods, it was added, vouchsafed the clearest signs of the favor with which they regarded the enterprise, and of the high destinies reserved for the young colony.

This event was likely to be a favorite theme of the old Latin minstrels. They would naturally attribute the project of Romulus to some divine intimation of the power and prosperity which it was decreed that his city should attain. They would probably introduce seers foretelling the victories of unborn consuls and dictators, and the last great victory would generally occupy the most conspicuous place in the prediction. There is nothing strange in the supposition that the poet who was employed to celebrate the first great triumph of the Romans over the Greeks might throw his song of exultation into this form.

The occasion was one likely to excite the strongest feelings of national pride. A great outrage had been followed by a great retribution. Seven years before this time, Lucius Posthumius Megellus, who sprang from one of the noblest houses of Rome, and had been thrice Consul, was sent ambassador to Tarentum, with charge to demand reparation for grievous injuries. The Tarentines gave him audience in their theatre, where he addressed them in such Greek as he could command, which, we may well believe, was not exactly such as Cineas would have spoken. An exquisite sense of the ridiculous belonged to the Greek character; and closely connected with this faculty was a strong propensity to flippancy and impertinence. When Posthumius placed an accent wrong, his hearers burst into a laugh. When he remonstrated, they hooted him, and called him a barbarian; and at length hissed him off the stage as if he had been a bad actor. As the grave Roman retired, a buffoon, who, from his constant drunkenness, was nicknamed the Pint Pot, came up with gestures of the grossest indecency, and bespattered the senatorial gown with filth. Posthumius turned round to the multitude, and held up the gown, as if appealing to the universal law of nations. The sight only increased the insolence of the Tarentines. They clapped their hands, and set up a shout of laughter which shook the theatre. " Men of Tarentum," said Posthumius, " It will take not a little blood to wash this gown."

Rome, in consequence of this insult, declared war against the Tarentines. The Tarentines sought for allies beyond the Ionian Sea. Pyrrhus, king of Epirus, came to their help with a large army; and, for the first time, the two great nations of antiquity were fairly matched against each other.

The fame of Greece in arms, as well as in arts, was then at the height. Half a century earlier, the career of Alexander had excited the admiration and terror of all nations from the Ganges to the Pillars of Hercules. Royal houses, founded by Macedonian captains, still

reigned at Antioch and Alexandria. That barbarian
warriors, led by barbarian chiefs, should win a pitched
battle against Greek valor guided by Greek science,
seemed as incredible as it would now seem that the Bur-
mese or the Siamese should, in the open plain, put to
flight an equal number of the best English troops. The
Tarentines were convinced that their countrymen were
irresistible in war ; and this conviction had emboldened
them to treat with the grossest indignity one whom they
regarded as the representative of an inferior race. Of
the Greek generals then living, Pyrrhus was indisput-
ably the first. Among the troops who were trained in
the Greek discipline, his Epirotes ranked high. His
expedition to Italy was a turning-point in the history of
the world. He found there a people who, far inferior
to the Athenians and Corinthians in the fine arts, in the
speculative sciences, and in all the refinements of life,
were the best soldiers on the face of the earth. Their
arms, their gradations of rank, their order of battle,
their method of intrenchment, were all of Latian origin,
and had all been gradually brought near to perfection,
not by the study of foreign models, but by the genius
and experience of many generations of great native
commanders. The first words which broke from the
king, when his practised eye had surveyed the Roman
encampment, were full of meaning : "These barba-
rians," he said, "have nothing barbarous in their mili-
tary arrangements." He was at first victorious ; for his
own talents were superior to those of the captains who
were opposed to him ; and the Romans were not pre-
pared for the onset of the elephants of the East, which
were then for the first time seen in Italy, — moving
mountains, with long snakes for hands. But the victo-

ries of the Epirotes were fiercely disputed, dearly pur·
chased, and altogether unprofitable. At length, Manius
Curius Dentatus, who had in his first consulship won
two triumphs, was again placed at the head of the Ro·
man Commonwealth, and sent to encounter the invaders.
A great battle was fought near Beneventum. Pyrrhus
was completely defeated. He repassed the sea; and
the world learned with amazement that a people had
been discovered who, in fair fighting, were 'superior to
the best troops that had been drilled on the system of
Parmenio and Antigonus.

The conquerors had a good right to exult in their suc-
cess, for their glory was all their own. They had not
learned from their enemy how to conquer him. It was
with their own national arms, and in their own national
battle array, that they had overcome weapons and tac-
tics long believed to be invincible. The pilum and the
broadsword had vanquished the Macedonian spear. The
legion had broken the Macedonian phalanx. Even the
elephants, when the surprise produced by their first ap-
pearance was over, could cause no disorder in the steady
yet flexible battalions of Rome.

It is said by Florus, and may easily be believed, that
the triumph far surpassed in magnificence any that
Rome had previously seen. The only spoils which Pa·
pirius Cursor and Fabius Maximus could exhibit were
flocks and herds, wagons of rude structure, and heaps
of spears and helmets. But now, for the first time, the
riches of Asia and the arts of Greece adorned a Roman
pageant. Plate, fine stuffs, costly furniture, rare ani-
mals, exquisite paintings and sculptures, formed part
of the procession. At the banquet would be assembled
ι crowd of warriors and statesmen, among whom Ma·

nius Curius Dentatus would take the highest room.
Caius Fabricius Luscinus, then, after two consulships
and two triumphs, Censor of the Commonwealth, would
doubtless occupy a place of honor at the board. In sit-
uations less conspicuous probably lay some of those who
were, a few years later, the terror of Carthage — Caius
Duilius, the founder of the maritime greatness of his
country ; Marcus Atilius Regulus, who owed to defeat a
renown far higher than that which he had derived from
his victories ; and Caius Lutatius Catulus, who, while
suffering from a grievous wound, fought the great battle
of the Ægates, and brought the First Punic War to
a triumphant close. It is impossible to recount the
names of these eminent citizens, without reflecting that
they were all, without exception, Plebeians, and would,
but for the ever-memorable struggle maintained by Caius
Licinius and Lucius Sextius, have been doomed to hide
in obscurity, or to waste in civil broils, the capacity and
energy which prevailed against Pyrrhus and Hamilcar.

On such a day we may suppose that the patriotic en-
thusiasm of a Latin poet would vent itself in reiterated
shouts of " Io Triumphe," such as were uttered by Horace
on a far less exciting occasion, and in boasts resembling
those which Virgil, two hundred and fifty years later,
put into the mouth of Anchises. The superiority of
some foreign nations, and especially of the Greeks, in
the lazy arts of peace, would be admitted with disdain-
ful candor ; but preëminence in all the qualities which
fit a people to subdue and govern mankind would be
claimed for the Romans.

The following lay belongs to the latest age of Latin
ballad-poetry. Nævius and Livius Andronicus were
probably among the children whose mothers held them

up to see the chariot of Curius go by. The minstrel who sang on that day might possibly have lived to read the first hexameters of Ennius, and to see the first comedies of Plautus. His poem, as might be expected, shows a much wider acquaintance with the geography, manners, and productions of remote nations than would have been found in compositions of the age of Camillus. But he troubles himself little about dates; and having heard travellers talk with admiration of the Colossus of Rhodes, and of the structures and gardens with which the Macedonian kings of Syria had embellished their residence on the banks of the Orontes, he has never thought of inquiring whether these things existed in the age of Romulus.

## THE PROPHECY OF CAPYS.

A LAY SUNG AT THE BANQUET IN THE CAPITOL, ON THE DAY WHEREON MANIUS CURIUS DENTATUS, A SECOND TIME CONSUL, TRIUMPHED OVER KING PYRRHUS AND THE TARENTINES, IN THE YEAR OF THE CITY CCCCLXXIX.

### 1

Now slain is King Amulius,
    Of the great Sylvian line,
Who reigned in Alba Longa,
    On the throne of Aventine.
5 Slain is the Pontiff Camers,
    Who spake the words of doom:

6. *The words of doom* to Rhea Ilia, or Sylvia, the daughter of Numitor, whose twin children, Romulus and Remus, were to be thrown into the Tiber, while the mother was buried alive.

"The children to the Tiber;
    The mother to the tomb."

### 2

In Alba's lake no fisher
10    His net to-day is flinging;
On the dark rind of Alba's oaks
    To-day no axe is ringing;
The yoke hangs o'er the manger;
    The scythe lies in the hay;
15 Through all the Alban villages
    No work is done to-day.

### 3

And every Alban burgher
    Hath donned his whitest gown;
And every head in Alba
20    Weareth a poplar crown;
And every Alban doorpost
    With boughs and flowers is gay;
For to-day the dead are living;
    The lost are found to-day.

### 4

25 They were doomed by a bloody king;
    They were doomed by a lying priest;
They were cast on the raging flood;
    They were tracked by the raging beast.
Raging beast and raging flood
30    Alike have spared the prey;
And to-day the dead are living;
    The lost are found to-day.

### 5

The troubled river knew them,
  And smoothed his yellow foam,
35 And gently rocked the cradle
  That bore the fate of Rome.
The ravening she-wolf knew them,
  And licked them o'er and o'er,
And gave them of her own fierce milk,
40  Rich with raw flesh and gore.
Twenty winters, twenty springs,
  Since then have rolled away;
And to-day the dead are living,
  The lost are found to-day.

### 6

45 Blithe it was to see the twins,
  Right goodly youths and tall,
Marching from Alba Longa
  To their old grandsire's hall.
Along their path fresh garlands
50  Are hung from tree to tree;
Before them stride the pipers,
  Piping a note of glee.

### 7

On the right goes Romulus,
  With arms to the elbows red,
55 And in his hand a broadsword,
  And on the blade a head, —
A head in an iron helmet,
  With horse-hair hanging down,
A shaggy head, a swarthy head,

60     Fixed in a ghastly frown,—
The head of King Amulius
    Of the great Sylvian line,
Who reigned in Alba Longa,
    On the throne of Aventine.

### 8

65 On the left side goes Remus,
    With wrists and fingers red,
And in his hand a boar-spear,
    And on the point a head, —
A wrinkled head and aged,
70     With silver beard and hair,
And holy fillets round it,
    Such as the pontiffs wear, —
The head of ancient Camers,
    Who spake the words of **doom:**
75 "The children to the Tiber;
    The mother to the tomb."

### 9

Two and two behind the twins
    Their trusty comrades go,
Four-and-forty valiant men,
80     With club, and axe, and bow.
On each side every hamlet
    Pours forth its joyous crowd,
Shouting lads and baying dogs
    And children laughing loud,
85 And old men weeping fondly
    As Rhea's boys go by,
And maids who shriek to see the heads,
    Yet, shrieking, press more nigh.

### 10

So they marched along the lake ;
**90**    They marched by fold and stall,
By cornfield and by vineyard,
Unto the old man's hall.

### 11

In the hall-gate sate Capys,
Capys, the sightless seer ;
**95** From head to foot he trembled
As Romulus drew near.
And up stood stiff his thin white hair,
And his blind eyes flashed fire :
"Hail ! foster-child of the wondrous nurse !
**200**    Hail ! son of the wondrous sire !

### 12

"But thou, — what dost thou here
In the old man's peaceful hall ?
What doth the eagle in the coop,
The bison in the stall ?
**105** Our corn fills many a garner ;
Our vines clasp many a tree ;
Our flocks are white on many a hill ;
But these are not for thee.

### 13

"For thee no treasure ripens
**210**    In the Tartessian mine :
For thee no ship brings precious bales

100. The god Mars was assumed to be the father of Romulus and Remus.
110. The *Tartessian mine* was the *Tarshish* of the Bible.

Across the Libyan brine;
Thou shalt not drink from amber;
Thou shalt not rest on down;
115 Arabia shall not steep thy locks,
Nor Sidon tinge thy gown.

### 14

" Leave gold and myrrh and jewels,
Rich table and soft bed,
To them who of man's seed are born,
120 Whom woman's milk have fed.
Thou wast not made for lucre,
For pleasure, nor for rest;
Thou, that art sprung from the War-god's loins,
And hast tugged at the she-wolf's breast.

### 15

125 " From sunrise unto sunset
All earth shall hear thy fame;
A glorious city thou shalt build,
And name it by thy name.
. And there, unquenched through ages,
130 Like Vesta's sacred fire,
Shall live the spirit of thy nurse,
The spirit of thy sire.

### 16

" The ox toils through the furrow,
Obedient to the goad;
135 The patient ass, up flinty paths,
Plods with his weary load;

112. Libya being northwestern Africa, the *Libyan brine* is the Mediterra
bean.

With whine and bound the spaniel
His master's whistle hears;
And the sheep yields her patiently
140   To the loud clashing shears.

### 17

" But thy nurse will hear no master;
Thy nurse will bear no load;
And woe to them that shear her,
And woe to them that goad!
145 When all the pack, loud baying,
Her bloody lair surrounds,
She dies in silence, biting hard,
Amidst the dying hounds.

### 18

" Pomona loves the orchard;
150   And Liber loves the vine;
And Pales loves the straw-built shed
Warm with the breath of kine;
And Venus loves the whispers
Of plighted youth and maid,
155 In April's ivory moonlight
Beneath the chestnut shade.

### 19

" But thy father loves the clashing
Of broadsword and of shield;
He loves to drink the steam that reeks
160   From the fresh battle-field

149. *Pomona* was the goddess of fruit.
150. *Liber*, or Bacchus.
151. *Pales* was a rustic divinity.

He smiles a smile more dreadful
    Than his own dreadful frown,
When he sees the thick black cloud of smoke
    Go up from the conquered town.

### 20

165 " And such as is the War-god,
    The author of thy line,
And such as she who suckled thee,
    Even such be thou and thine.
Leave to the soft Campanian
170    His baths and his perfumes;
Leave to the sordid race of Tyre
    Their dyeing-vats and looms:
Leave to the sons of Carthage
    The rudder and the oar:
175 Leave to the Greek his marble Nymphs
    And scrolls of wordy lore.

### 21

" Thine, Roman, is the pilum;
    Roman, the sword is thine,
The even trench, the bristling mound,
180    The legion's ordered line;
And thine the wheels of triumph,
    Which with their laurelled train
Move slowly up the shouting streets
    To Jove's eternal fane.

169. The inhabitants of the Campania, the fertile district below Latium, yielded to the seductions of an unwarlike life.
171. The Tyrians were occupied only with manufactures and commerce.
173. The Carthaginians had the carrying trade of the Old World.
177. The *pilum* was the long Roman spear.

### 22

185 " Beneath thy yoke the Volscian
      Shall veil his lofty brow;
    Soft Capua's curled revellers
      Before thy chairs shall bow;
    The Lucumoes of Arnus
190   Shall quake thy rods to see;
    And the proud Samnite's heart of steel
      Shall yield to only thee.

### 23

    " The Gaul shall come against thee
      From the land of snow and night;
195 Thou shalt give his fair-haired armies
      To the raven and the kite.

### 24

    " The Greek shall come against thee,
      The conqueror of the East.
    Beside him stalks to battle
200   The huge earth-shaking beast,
    The beast on whom the castle
      With all its guards doth stand,
    The beast who hath between his eyes
      The serpent for a hand.
205 First march the bold Epirotes,
      Wedged close with shield and spear;
    And the ranks of false Tarentum
      Are glittering in the rear.

---

193. The prediction points to the invasion by the Gauls under Brennus.
197. The Greek invader is Pyrrhus, king of Epeiros.
200. Pyrrhus made use of the elephant.

### 25

" The ranks of false Tarentum
210 Like hunted sheep shall fly ;
In vain the bold Epirotes
 Shall round their standards die.
And Apennine's gray vultures
 Shall have a noble feast
215 On the fat and the eyes
 Of the huge earth-shaking beast.

### 26

" Hurrah ! for the good weapons
 That keep the War-god's land.
Hurrah ! for Rome's stout pilum
220 In a stout Roman hand.
Hurrah ! for Rome's short broadsword,
 That through the thick array
Of levelled spears and serried shields
 Hews deep its gory way.

### 27

225 " Hurrah ! for the great triumph
 That stretches many a mile.
Hurrah ! for the wan captives
 That pass in endless file.
Ho ! bold Epirotes, whither
230 Hath the Red King ta'en flight?
Ho ! dogs of false Tarentum,
 Is not the gown washed white ?

### 28

" Hurrah ! for the great triumph
 That stretches many a mile.

230. The word *Pyrrhus* means red.

235 Hurrah! for the rich dye of Tyre,
        And the fine web of Nile,
    The helmets gay with plumage
        Torn from the pheasant's wings,
    The belts set thick with starry gems
240     That shone on Indian kings,
    The urns of massy silver,
        The goblets rough with gold,
    The many-colored tablets bright
        With loves and wars of old,
245 The stone that breathes and struggles,
        The brass that seems to speak, —
    Such cunning they who dwell on high
        Have given unto the Greek.


### 29

    "Hurrah! for Manius Curius,
250     The bravest son of Rome,
    Thrice in utmost need sent forth,
        Thrice drawn in triumph home.
    Weave, weave for Manius Curius
        The third embroidered gown:
255 Make ready the third lofty car,
        And twine the third green crown;
    And yoke the steeds of Rosea
        With necks like a bended bow,
    And deck the bull, Mevania's bull,
260     The bull as white as snow.


### 30

    " Blest and thrice blest the Roman
        Who sees Rome's brightest day,
    Who sees that long victorious pomp

Wind down the Sacred Way,
255 And through the bellowing Forum
And round the Suppliant's Grove,
Up to the everlasting gates
Of Capitolian Jove.

31

" Then where, o'er two bright havens,
270     The towers of Corinth frown ;
Where the gigantic King of Day
On his own Rhodes looks down ;
Where soft Orontes murmurs
Beneath the laurel shades ;
275 Where Nile reflects the endless length
Of dark-red colonnades ;
Where in the still deep water,
Sheltered from waves and blasts,
Bristles the dusky forests
280     Of Byrsa's thousand masts ;
Where fur-clad hunters wander
Amidst the northern ice ;
Where through the sand of morning-land
The camel bears the spice ;
285 Where Atlas flings his shadow
Far o'er the western foam, —
Shall be great fear on all who hear
The mighty name of Rome."

271. The gigantic Colossus of Rhodes, which was a statue to the sun god.
273. The city of Antioch was on the banks of the *Orontes.*
280. Byrsa, the Biblical Bozra, was the citadel of Carthage.
285. The reference is to the great mountain range of northwestern Africa

# CHRONOLOGY OF ANCIENT ROME
## DOWN TO THE SACK BY THE GAULS
### *According to the Roman Legend.*

B. C.

753   Rome founded by *Romulus* and *Remus*, grandsons of King Numitor of Alba Longa. Remus slain in a quarrel.

753–716   Romulus, King of Rome.

715–673   Numa Pompilius.

673–641   Tullus Hostilius.

641–616   Ancus Marcius.

616–578   Tarquinius Priscus.

578–534   Servius Tullius.

534–510   Tarquinius Superbus.

510   Rape of Lucretia by Sextus, the king's son, followed by her suicide. The agitation caused by this resulted in the expulsion of the king and the abolition of the monarchy.

509   Rome becomes a republic under two consuls.

508   War with the Etruscan king Porsena of Clusium. *Horatius Cocles* defends the bridge over the Tiber.

496   Great victory of the Romans over the Latins by the small *Lake Regillus* near Tusculum.

494   Secession of the Plebeians or common people from the city until placated by the creation of plebeian tribunes to represent them in the government.

451   Ten men called Decemvirs placed at the head of the government.

450   Under the leadership of Appius Claudius the Decemvirs refuse to retire when their term ends. The stabbing of *Virginia* (whose honor Appius Claudius had threatened) by her father results in an uprising which obliges the Decemvirs to abdicate.

390   Gauls under Brennus win the battle of the Allia and sack the city of Rome except the Capitoline hill.

(For further details see Ploetz's Epitome of History, translated by Tillinghast, pages 87–100.)

# HISTORY

## Ancient History

The Story of the Greek People.  By EVA MARCH TAPPAN.  $ .65

The Story of the Roman People.  By EVA MARCH TAPPAN.  .65

## European History

A History of Mediæval and Modern Europe, for Secondary Schools.  By WILLIAM STEARNS DAVIS.  Assisted by NORMAN S. McKENDRICK.  1.50

European Hero Stories.  By EVA MARCH TAPPAN.  .65

Old World Hero Stories.  By EVA MARCH TAPPAN.  .70

## English History

England's Story.  By EVA MARCH TAPPAN.  A History of England for Grammar and High Schools.  .85

History of England.  By J. N. LARNED.  1.25

Ireland's Story.  By CHARLES JOHNSTON and CARITA SPENCER.  *School Edition*.  1.10

## United States History

*The Houghton Mifflin Textbooks in United States History for Elementary Schools.*

Book I.  An Elementary History of Our Country.  By EVA MARCH TAPPAN.  .65

Book II.  History of the United States for Grammar Schools.  By R. G. THWAITES and C. N. KENDALL.  1.00

---

American Hero Stories.  By EVA MARCH TAPPAN.  .55

A History of the United States for Schools.  By JOHN FISKE.  1.00

A History of the United States.  For Secondary Schools.  By J. N. LARNED.  1.40

*Prices are net, postpaid.*

---

## HOUGHTON MIFFLIN COMPANY
BOSTON  NEW YORK  CHICAGO
1411